'A blazing, unlikely tri[...]
idea of a hero.' *The Ne[w ...]*

Controversial and [...]
infamous Larry Flynt's li[fe ...]
make it one of the most interesting life stories of our time. He
is this century's most ardent advocate of First Amendment
rights, a man whose landmark Supreme Court cases are studied
by every law student in America. He is the pivotal character in
an ongoing feminist debate on pornography, a man who marks
the boundary between opposing camps within the movement.
He is a twentieth-century, blue collar Rabelais who has
mocked religious hypocrisy with an acid tongue and a biting
wit. He is the founder of *Hustler* magazine, a journal often
described as tasteless, crude, scatological, and gynaecologically
explicit —to which he would reply, 'Good!' For Flynt,
tastelessness is 'a necessary tool in challenging preconceived
notions in a world where people are afraid to discuss their
attitudes, prejudices, and misconceptions.'

Larry Flynt is a person for whom the term 'colourful' is
completely inadequate. Born in the hills of Kentucky, in the
poorest county in America, Flynt became a teenage runaway,
an underage recruit in both the army and the navy, a
bootlegger, a scam artist, a bar owner, the proprietor of a string
of go-go clubs, an evangelical Christian, an atheist, and
eventually a millionaire pornographer and publisher. A
prodigious sexual athlete, Flynt was shot down in his prime by
an assailant's bullet and paralysed from the waist down.

Wheelchair bound and racked by years of searing pain,
he became a pain-medicine junkie and habitué of America's
courtrooms. Persecuted by the self-righteous Charles Keating,
prosecuted by ambitious district attorneys, sued by moral
crusaders like Jerry Falwell, and hounded by the government,
Flynt forged a blazing trail through the American legal system.
Even the most straightforward journalistic account of his life
would make engrossing reading. His story, never told before, is
an American drama.

An Unseemly Man

Larry Flynt

with Kenneth Ross

BLOOMSBURY

First published in the USA by Dove Books 1996

This paperback edition first published 1997

Copyright © 1996 by Larry Flynt

The moral right of the author has been asserted

Bloomsbury Publishing Plc, 38 Soho Square, London W1V 5DF

A CIP catalogue record for this book
is available from the British Library

10 9 8 7 6 5 4 3 2 1

ISBN 0 7475 3398 9

Printed in Great Britain by Cox & Wyman Ltd, Reading

To Althea

Contents

Foreword

→

WHO IS LARRY FLYNT?

• FOUR POINTS OF VIEW •

Larry Flynt has lived a life of classic highs and lows that few men in our age will ever come close to experiencing. I suppose he is the late twentieth-century version of Horatio Alger pursuing the American Dream, but with the perverse twist of building his empire from pornography. And like most men who succeed based on fierce determination and moral ambiguity, he draws judgments as extreme as the highs and lows he has lived. For this reason I find him personally to be more in the rapscallion tradition of Mark Twain's Huckleberry Finn—the country boy, misunderstood by so many, trying to figure it all out, rafting down the American psyche of a country gone wacko. Larry, by some standards, is a First Amendment hero and defender of the Constitution; he is also an exploiter of women and a one-man wrecking crew on "community standards." Does he fight the dirty fight for us, or does he care only about a buck, as the head of a sleazy media empire that hides behind a cause? Therein lies the reason Larry Flynt is fascinating. When you actually step inside his life, as we tried to do in our movie, you navigate a minefield of contradictions.

On one hand, Larry Flynt was raised dirt poor in a one-room shack in Kentucky. On the other, he knows what it is to have more money than he could ever spend. He has had sex both with a chicken and with some of the world's most beautiful women. He has been a fervent born-again Christian and a reckless atheist. He has lived a pagan, orgiastic lifestyle, but he has also had to contend with being paralyzed in the prime of his life. He has been railroaded and jailed by the justice system, but he has also had his most noble triumph in the halls of the Supreme Court, in one of the finest hours of recent American legal history. He is someone desperately trying to obtain a certain respect, but he is also hopelessly tethered by his crude roots and the derivation of his wealth. And finally, while he has known the great power of running an empire, he has also known the hopelessness of watching the true love of his life suffer from AIDS and eventually die of a drug overdose.

From my personal experience with Larry Flynt, I get the sense of someone still a little stunned by everything that has happened to him; someone still looking back, in the last act of his life, at the good and the bad, with a strange recognition of the painful wisdom his experiences have given him. He's had his fair share of life—poverty, jail, drug addiction, and a partly successful assassination attempt—and he's also had great joy. I'm not sure where he stands on it all, because life, for people who live passionately, tends in the end to be an overwhelmingly vast and neutral canvas that renders no final decision, no sense of win or lose. I sometimes even get the feeling that if Larry could rewind his life and edit it like a home movie, there is a bitter wisdom within that would not allow him to change anything.

Is Larry Flynt a hero? Not in the classic cinematic sense. Hardly. But is there not another definition of heroism? I think of Ron Kovic, who lived in the same era and wrote *Born on the Fourth of July*, which I adapted into a movie. Kovic came to understand, in the end, that the definition of a hero is a shifting one, and very often where we end up has very little resemblance to where we started. Screenwriters Larry Karaszewski and Scott Alexander, and our director, Milos Forman, have very much grappled with the question of who Larry Flynt really is. The answer, I believe, as with many of us, lies in the contradictions—and so to judge him by community standards or conformism, or small thinking, is to face a hopeless conundrum. He has helped us all as Americans by scapegoating himself, and as we know, those people who speak the loudest in any age are often the most condemned—until history, on its own eccentric path, discovers them years later. As you look into Larry Flynt's life, look at it, if nothing else, as an examination of the extremes of the human experience;

try to empathize as a fellow traveler with his suffering and his triumph. And there, I believe, you will discover the real relevance of his story.

—Oliver Stone
Producer, *The People vs. Larry Flynt*
Santa Monica, California

✗ ✗ ✗

I am definitely one of those old-fashioned, small-town people who was conditioned, in my childhood in Czechoslovakia, to think that pornography is bad, and—I am afraid—I shall never be able to shake off this notion.

So the only reason I consented to read a script about Larry Flynt was as a courtesy to Oliver Stone, who figured as producer on the project. After I had turned the last page, to my shock and in contravention of my childhood conditioning, I knew I wanted—and had—to make this film.

Twice in my life I have had the misfortune to live in societies where freedom of expression was totally suppressed, and where open discourse was an illegal act: first under the Nazis, and then the Communists. I have seen the devastating effect these repressive measures had on the quality of life. Boredom ruled everyone except those in power and those who were marching to the gallows.

I think it significant that both these regimes started with crusades against those they classified as perverts: pornographers, homosexuals, Jews, and blacks. As time went by, the list grew longer and longer, until one day it included Shakespeare, Jesus Christ, Mark Twain, and William Faulkner; and finally, any plumber, teacher, or housewife who did not conform to the official ideology. Perverts all.

I must admit that I have never bought *Hustler* magazine, and I believe I never will. But as long as I live, I will always admire Larry Flynt: his life, his courage, and his tenacity. Less surprisingly, the Supreme Court of the United States is and will always be my hero.

—Milos Forman
Director, *The People vs. Larry Flynt*
New York, New York

✗ ✗ ✗

I remember Bryan Lourd giving me a script called *The People vs. Larry Flynt,* and telling me that the great Milos Forman was interested in having me play the title role. Before I read it, I asked *the* question, the one I have heard asked many times since: "Why would anyone want to make a movie about him?" Bryan said, "Woody, it's Milos Forman. Read it." So I read it and liked it, but wasn't at all satisfied. I was living near Cincinnati when his trial was going on, and shared the opinion of most everyone else in my church-influenced environment: Larry Flynt was a scumbag! Why does he deserve a movie? Then I watched a documentary about him and was struck by his sense of humor and charisma.

But most of all, I was struck by what he was saying: If the First Amendment did not protect him, it did not protect anyone. Is it possible that the First Amendment freedoms we enjoy today exist only through the considerable efforts of a lowly pornographer? The more I learned about Larry's life, the more intrigued I became.

When I went to meet Larry in his offices in Beverly Hills, I was nervous. I didn't know what to expect. I had heard he was not terribly coherent because of prescription drug use, and of course, he had been confined to a wheelchair for nearly twenty years. What had paralysis done to this man who drew so much of his vitality from the waist down? While waiting outside his office, I was surprised by the way everything was decorated. The place had a very conservative, expensive, almost Victorian flavor to it. Quite a contrast to the humble beginnings of a man who grew up in the hills of Kentucky "so far back in the hollow we had to pipe in sunshine." In fact, one of the things that I found intriguing about Larry was the fact that both of us were poor white trash who somehow got a leg up in the world. When I was summoned and walked in, I found him on the other side of an enormous office, behind a huge desk, seated in a gold wheelchair. He greeted me in his slow, raspy eastern Kentucky drawl, which I would subsequently spend many hours trying to duplicate.

I asked Larry many questions, getting increasingly personal as the interview progressed, and began to realize why this man deserved to have a movie made about his life. The reasons go well beyond his passionate defense of freedom of the press. Larry is human, and it is always refreshing to discover the humanity in someone we have demonized. Larry is as vulnerable as anyone I've ever met because of the unfettered way he expresses himself. How often do you say exactly what you feel without censoring yourself, and without worrying about what others might think? Larry does not censor himself, and rightfully believes our government shouldn't do so, either. Granted, his outspoken honesty has gotten him into a lot of trouble. He has spent millions in the last twenty years defending himself in court. But he loves to stir things up and to jolt people out of their lethargy.

Well, I can't wait to read the book you're holding, but I will also be very interested to see the chapters not yet written. I don't know what drives this man, but when you have finished his autobiography, you might believe with me that there is plenty of fight left in him. You haven't heard the last of Larry Flynt.

—Woody Harrelson
Actor, *The People vs. Larry Flynt*
Los Angeles, California

x x x

Larry Flynt is a monster and a madman. He is a monster to those who hate freedom and a madman in pursuit of his own freedom.

I first met Larry a quarter century ago, when the sexual landscape was quite different than it is today.

The American libido was still firmly chained in its backyard, hidden from company as if it were a cretinous child. People were still coy talking about sex in public. Abuse, incest, and rape were dirty little secrets, which "propriety" helped keep hidden.

"Good poets borrow, great poets steal," said T. S. Eliot. By this measure, Larry Flynt is a great poet. He freely admits he stole part of *Hustler*'s format from my magazine, *Screw*. He went on to steal my defense lawyers and one of my best editors. But that is all to Larry's credit. He is the most determined bulldog I've ever known.

Larry has made a success of virtually everything he has attempted, and he has done it with integrity and consistency. He absolutely refuses to permit anyone to censor any word or thought; more important, he refuses to censor himself.

Larry Flynt is my role model. His extraordinary Supreme Court victory in the Jerry Falwell satire case set one of the most important legal precedents of the twentieth century. He is always there to remind us not to take sex too seriously.

I salute Larry Flynt as a publishing genius and as a sexual warrior. With this book and with the film *The People vs. Larry Flynt*, maybe, finally, possibly, this brilliant man will get the recognition he deserves.

—Al Goldstein
Publisher, *Screw* Magazine
New York, New York

An Unseemly Man

1.
Playing Chicken

IT IS A BLUSTERY WINTER DAY, AND THE VIEW FROM *my office is spectacular. Behind me to the north are the Hollywood Hills, where the white dome of Griffith Park Observatory gleams in the afternoon sun. To my right the city unfolds west toward the ocean. On my left the modest skyline of Los Angeles gives way to the San Gabriel Mountains, high above Pasadena. My office is ten stories above Beverly Hills: a luxurious, glass-walled enclave. I am sitting in a gold-plated wheelchair in custom-made clothes behind a massive, hand-carved desk flanked by two priceless Tiffany lamps. My limousine and Bentley sedan are parked downstairs. The name on the top of the building is my own. My Hollywood Hills estate is a few miles to the west. My Gulfstream jet is parked in a nearby hangar, its crew ready to take me anywhere I want to go.*

My office is quiet today; the only sound I can hear is the air conditioning cycling on and off. It is Saturday, and the halls outside are dark and empty. It's a good time to think. How did I get here? Who am I? In one sense I am the real Beverly Hillbilly, but unlike the fictional

Clampetts, I have left an indelible imprint on American society. I am only fifty-three years old. Long after their reruns have ended, the effects of my tumultuous career will continue. But was it worth it? My career cost me the use of my legs. It may have cost the life of my wife, Althea. I have been reviled, prosecuted, imprisoned, and shot. I have spent half my life, it seems, in court. I have survived years of the worst physical pain any human can endure. I have accomplished much and triumphed against the odds. But one thing I have not done. I have not looked back. I couldn't; I was too busy living life. Perhaps it is time.

x x x

I was born in Lakeville, a tiny, isolated community in the hills of Magoffin County in eastern Kentucky. The old hillbillies referred to the area by its original, more colorful designation: *Lickskillet.* In the Appalachian tongue, Lakeville was a *holler* or "hollow"—a small valley scooped out of the ancient, wooded hills of the Cumberland Mountains. It was a long, narrow place that wound westward from an intersection of similar valleys near the township of Salyersville. Each side of the hollow was intersected by smaller ones: a whole network of cracks and crevices. Unlike the arid Hollywood Hills behind me, the hill country of Kentucky is a rugged maze of streams, rivers, and rain-drenched valleys. When I was growing up, its steep ridges and deep hollows were carpeted with trees, populated with a host of small animals, and home to only a few scattered families. It was a long way from Beverly Hills, California.

As you moved toward Lakeville, you met grimy coal trucks groaning down steep mountain roads, carrying their dusty cargo from remote mines to railheads and processing plants. A few brick houses stood near the highways in stark contrast to the scores of dilapidated wooden shacks, half-collapsed barns, and outhouses of my hollow. Many wooden dwellings were relics built before the turn of the century. The oldest homes occupied the rich bottomland alongside streams that descended from the green glades above.

The hills around Lakeville defined the landscape and shaped my psyche in profound ways, but their beauty hid the squalor in which I lived. When I was growing up, Magoffin County was the poorest in America. Hill people like me were isolated by dirt roads: We lacked television, household appliances, and common consumer goods—nearly everything Americans took for granted. We were cut off from the outside world: a small, gritty, insular band of people.

The twentieth century did not begin to reach the hill country of eastern Kentucky until the early 1950s. I was nearly ten years old before any of the roads were paved. Before then even horse-drawn wagons could not negotiate the muddy ruts and washes of Lakeville's dirt roads. Life was simple, and opportunities for entertainment were extremely limited. This isolation was the seedbed of alcoholism. Hard drinking was a cardinal trait of hill folk, part of the social landscape.

People had little else to do. Many drank their lives away in quiet desperation, blaming their weakness on the fact that Magoffin County was "dry." "If we could get liquor any time we wanted it, and drink it openly and at our leisure, we wouldn't have this problem," they would say. There was no Alcoholics Anonymous or anything like it in the hollow. Any excuse to get drunk went unchallenged. It was an ingrained characteristic of the culture. Illicit whiskey bootlegged in, or "white lightning" brewed farther back in the hills, had been a major industry since the area was first settled. But most people controlled their consumption enough to be productive. With a perverse kind of discipline, folks postponed their binges until the weekends, staying sober during the week so they could complete those chores necessary for survival.

Most of my neighbors were completely ignorant of the outside world. Often illiterate, folks could not or did not read and may not have traveled more than a few miles in their entire lives. In its seclusion Lakeville was like a medieval settlement. And like a relic from the Middle Ages, a strong tradition of storytelling and rhyme survived in the speech and mannerisms of my neighbors. I remember one old lady who used to sell apples at a riverside clearing near the general store. Before attempting to ford the swift-moving current one day, a man on the other side called to her and asked, "What time is it? How deep's the river? What price are yer apples?" Without hesitation, she answered in verse:

[4]

Half past eight
Not quite nine
Up to your ass
Three for a dime.

I remember that same woman's reaction to her first sighting of an airplane. An old biplane flew over one day when I was a child, the sound of its big radial engine bouncing off the sides of the hollow. It was the first airplane she had ever seen, and it frightened the wits out of her. She dropped to her knees and began praying, "Oh, Lord! I knew you was comin' but I din't know 'twas goin' to be so soon!" She thought that airplane was God's chariot. She had never heard of the Wright Brothers, much less Pan Am. For her and other old-time residents, that little general store was the limit of their universe, and that universe was very, very small. Until the 1950s Lakeville looked like an old sepia-tone photograph. Hillbillies in faded, worn-out clothes used to tie up their horses at the hitching post in front. In the summer, old men sat on the porch, whittling. In winter, wizened old patriarchs sat around a potbellied stove and played checkers. It was a different world. It was my world.

The first Flynt in Magoffin County was my great-great-grandfather, John Flynt II, who was born in Scott County, West Virginia. In 1828, at the age of nineteen, he moved to our secluded hollow with his new bride, a Scottish girl named Fada McFarland. They settled in and with heroic effort carved a niche in the wilderness.

[5]

A miller and carpenter, John Flynt set up a furniture workshop and gristmill where a stream emptied into Lickin' River. The stream has been known as Flynt Branch ever since. My great-grandfather Miles, a carpenter and blacksmith, was born in the family home on Flynt Branch and lived there until his death in 1918. My grandfather Ernest was also a carpenter and blacksmith but later became a schoolteacher. He built the first schoolhouse in Lakeville with his own hands, a one-room building that served generations of Lakeville children. By the time I was born, four generations of my family had already lived in that hollow. Over the years they married into other pioneer families, including the Arnetts, the Hoskins, and the Fairchilds. I am related to most of the old-time residents.

When I was growing up, Lakeville had a population of about forty, made up of four or five families. The entire county had a population of less than five hundred. Most people were self-sufficient, raising corn, vegetables, hogs, chickens, cows (for beef, milk, and butter), and tobacco. The focal point of the scattered cabins, shacks, and farmhouses of the hollow—and the only commercial enterprise within its tight geographical boundaries—was that tiny general store. My family went there to buy necessities like salt and sugar, but just as importantly, we dropped by to share news and tell stories.

Like most folk in the hollow, we had a highly developed sense of history, and a certain fatalism, too. This was expressed in conversations at the store and at home. We took extraordinary pride in the skills, hard

[6]

work, and accomplishments of our families, past and present, and we were acutely aware of being different from "flatland" people. My grandparents were my link to the past and among the last generation of that special breed of men and women who originally colonized the hills. My neighbors were simple, practical folk, their outlook on life shaped by the confines of the mountains that limited both their movement and ambition. Some were slow-thinking and slow-moving, but most were filled with a store of common sense and a deep understanding of life rooted in the mineral-rich soil of Appalachia.

I was born at home in Lakeville on November 1, 1942, to Claxton Flynt and Edith Arnett. A few weeks after my birth, my father, who had been drafted into the army, was shipped to the South Pacific. It was the first time he had ever left the hollow. He did not return until October 1945. My father was a stranger to me when he returned. He neither held me as an infant nor witnessed my first step. In fact, my father was perpetually out of step and out of place, absent even when he was present. Often in trouble as a boy, he somehow successfully wooed my mother. They were married the year before I was born. Always a heavy drinker, he returned to the bottle within a few months after coming home from the Pacific. The slow pace of life in the hills was unbearable to him. My folks never really had a honeymoon—much less a chance to succeed—and his return from combat immediately plunged them into a warfare of their own. When my dad was able to get a job—which was rare—and keep it for any time, he drank up most or all of his paychecks.

In 1946 my parents had a second child, my sister, Judy. Two years later my brother, Jimmy, was born. Of the two, I was closer to my sister. I took pride in caring for her and acting the part of big brother and protector. But the closeness did not last long. Judy died of leukemia in 1951. The details of her death are unclear to me now. Only the pain is still vivid. I was very young. She died a pathetic little figure in a tiny rural hospital. My large extended family stood by her during a protracted death vigil. She slipped away one day while I stood by, helpless and sad. I did not realize at the time that Judy's death was to be the first in a series of losses for me.

The following year my parents separated. Our little family had been disbanded by death and divorce. I was barely eleven years old. I went with my mother to Hamlet, Indiana, where she had found a job as a waitress. Jimmy was taken in by our paternal grandmother, Lizzie. From that time forward Jimmy and I spent most of our young lives apart, bouncing around among different relatives. I would not see him again until he was a teenager.

With the eyes of an adult I can look back and see the sadness and brokenness that characterized my childhood. But for the most part, my memories of that time are not painful. My self-perception was not shaped by any consciousness of alienation or emotional loss. Some might see my childhood as tragic. Perhaps it was, but I've never dwelled much on it. Hill people like me have a highly developed sense of fate. We just accept things. Our sense of tradition, our knack for telling stories, our feeling of connection with kin is offset, I suppose, by a certain reluctance to personalize history. As a child, I didn't keep a journal or a diary or any such thing. Consequently, my memory is incomplete, a patchwork of images and impressions. Perhaps what I've forgotten is as significant as what I remember.

My earliest recollections go back to when I was three years old, long before my parents' divorce. I have a vivid memory of a time when my cousin and I were playing near one of two tobacco barns next to my grandma Arnett's house. It was fall, and a chill wind was stripping the trees of their autumn leaves and cutting right through my thin clothes. Seeking shelter, we went into the barn. Above our heads hung row after row of tobacco, an upside-down garden of leaves and stalks skewered on sticks and suspended between the rafters. It smelled like the inside of a humidor. Shivering in my overalls and cotton shirt, I gathered a few sticks of wood, determined to make a fire. At age three my fire-making skills exceeded my judgment by a wide margin. I expertly arranged the kindling as every hill-child could, lit it with a match, and added the scraps of wood I had found. For a few moments my cousin and I enjoyed the warmth. I never thought to look up until I heard the crackle and felt the heat. The sparks had risen to the racks of tobacco overhead. In an instant the little fire had become a conflagration.

We fled. Midway through the blaze the heat became so intense that it caused an explosion that blew off the roof, depositing it on top of a nearby hill. In later years I came to think of that event as a metaphor for my life. I've unintentionally blown the roof off of social and political institutions, too. I still like to play with fire.

My first sexual experience, far more comic than erotic, came at a very young age. It happened one day when my mother, father, grandparents, and neighbors were slaughtering hogs. Most people would not consider this annual rite an ideal prelude to sex. Slaughtering hogs was a process that involved shooting them in the head, hanging them up by the heels, slitting their throats to bleed them, and pouring boiling water over the carcasses so the bristles could be scraped off. The stench of scalded hog is pungent and would gag most city folks. The next step wouldn't be considered a turn-on, either. The animals would then be butchered and the meat hung in the smokehouse to cure. Smoked meat did not require refrigeration, something few people had at the time. Slaughtering hogs was a community event held every fall. Although the adults were well entertained—for them it was a party—I'd seen this done every year since I was born and soon grew bored. It had been four years since my accidental arson. I was seven. Seeking a diversion, I went up into a nearby hollow with two girls—a cousin about my age and a neighbor girl, Imogene. Imogene was about thirteen and a budding pubescent.

When we had arrived at a secluded spot, my cousin asked me if I wanted to "do it" with Imogene, "like the grown-ups do." Imogene was the picture of seduction in a dirty, loose-fitting, hand-me-down dress. Even so, I didn't know what she was talking about, so she graciously offered to demonstrate. Unceremoniously lying down on the ground, she pulled her skirt up and panties down. Having done so, she revealed her beautiful olive skin and a wisp of silky-black pubic hair. The eroticism of the moment was lost on me. While my bemused cousin watched, Imogene instructed me to take my pants off and get on top of her. She played with my penis for a while, and I did a lot of squirming and humping as she instructed. My prepubescent erection was not up to the task, however. I never did enter her, and of course I didn't have an orgasm, but I sure thought I'd "done it." After we got dressed and brushed ourselves off, we went back down to my grandparents' house, where everyone was still butchering hogs. I sidled up to my father, hooked my thumbs in my overalls, stuck my chest out, and said, "Betcha can't guess what I just did." "What?" my father asked. "I just fucked Imogene!" I replied, with a proud look on my face. My father stood there with an amused grin, saying nothing. My mother overheard the whole thing, however, and was not pleased. The next thing I knew, she was slapping my ears and herding me toward the house. I probably wouldn't remember it so well except that my dad kidded me about it for years.

In spite of that inauspicious beginning, all my friends and associates agree, without reservation, that I have always had a voracious appetite for sex. I usually describe my sexual proclivities as pedestrian, and although my sexual behavior has ranged over the years from the bizarre to the heroic, only one of my early experiences could actually be considered "deviant." This was the occasion when, at the age of nine, I had sex with a chicken. Yes, this is what the old preachers called bestiality. In the hollows of eastern Kentucky it wasn't all that unusual. Sexual relations with animals—particularly cows, sheep, and horses—were common. Some of the older boys in the area told me that a chicken was as good as a girl—that its egg bag was "hot as a girl's pussy" and "chickens wiggled around a lot more." In fact, they added, it was better in some ways because you could just grab the first chicken that came by—no wooing, no waiting. Anxious to experiment, I caught one of my grandmother's hens out behind the barn, managed to insert my penis into its egg bag, and thrust away. When I let the chicken go, it started toward the main house, staggering, squawking, and bleeding. Fearing that my grandmother would see the hen and want to know what had happened, I caught it and wrung its neck, then threw the bird in the creek. I decided that I liked girls better.

A rite of passage for hill-country boys was the gift of a gun. I grew up with guns, and they have played a significant and sometimes violent role in my life. The country folk of eastern Kentucky have traditionally regarded firearms as a natural extension of their personal power. I got my first gun, a .22-caliber rifle, when I was about eight. Like other boys who grew up in the hills, I used it to hunt rabbits and squirrels and shoot fish in the shallow waters of Lickin' River. On one occasion I used it for another purpose. I must have been about ten years old, and was already an experienced hunter. My father, not a man of patience with man or beast, ordered me to put an unwanted cat in a gunnysack, take it to the river, and drown it. I was reluctant, but, following orders, I threw the sacked cat into the river. Somehow the feisty thing got loose and began swimming to shore. I had my rifle with me. Knowing I would get a beating if the cat made it back to the house, I shot it to death. That was the last thing I ever killed. It haunts me even today. Before that time, I used to shoot small animals for food without remorse. After killing that cat, though, something changed. It was like a premonition. I couldn't shoot at any creature.

After my parents' divorce I moved out of my Kentucky hollow to urban Indiana. It was a transitional time for me emotionally. In my growing self-awareness I did not like myself much. As a young boy I was mottled with freckles, possessed an unruly shock of curly red hair, was chubby, and had a bulldog face. But I was too young to notice, and people didn't much care what you looked like in the hills. In Indiana, a more civilized place, I felt self-conscious. I had slimmed down, but still thought my head looked too big for my body and that my freckles and red hair looked silly. I felt ugly and thought girls would never find me attractive. Furthermore, I was bothered by an inability to express the complex thoughts and impressions that flooded my active mind. I was limited by the peculiar syntax of a hill-country youth. But within the limits of my age, vocabulary, and experience, I began to fantasize about the future and started to dream big dreams. I retreated inside my mind and became quiet and reserved. Instead of joining other kids in play, I became serious-minded, living out the dreams in my head. I either worked to earn money or sought the solace of my own company, keeping busy delivering newspapers and performing odd jobs. Somehow I managed to complete the fifth and sixth grades, even though I considered school an inconvenience.

In the meantime my mother remarried. I was miserable. I didn't like Indiana, my school, or my new step-father. I complained all the time. Finally I convinced my exasperated, worn-down mother to let me go back to Kentucky. During summer vacation, arrangements were made for me to stay with my Aunt Mary, whose husband had recently suffered a stroke. The couple owned a farm on the outskirts of Salyersville. I was to pay for my room and board by taking care of the live-stock and helping out on the farm. And so with some sense of relief, I returned to Kentucky. I finished the seventh and eighth grades in Salyersville, graduated from junior high, and entered high school in the fall of 1955. I made average grades but was an indifferent stu-dent, preferring instead to daydream. But I did not find happiness in Salyersville, either. These were hard years for me. My father was still an alcoholic, often going on benders that would last unabated for months.

My mother had left the hollow under a cloud of sala-cious rumors. I was alone with an elderly aunt and a disabled uncle. I had to work long hours each week, plowing fields, while looking up a mule's ass. I still had nothing. I was embarrassed and ashamed: of my parents, of myself, of my life. My unhappiness finally overwhelmed me.

During the spring of my freshman year, I decided to run away. I intended to go to Ohio and find work. I caught a bus in Salyersville that took me as far as West Liberty, and then began hitchhiking. I was eventually picked up by a man in a sweat-soaked shirt and shiny, dark-colored suit. He flashed a badge and claimed to be a police officer. There was a two-way radio in his '53 Chevy, and he had a .38-caliber revolver tucked into a holster on his belt. The man told me he was looking for a runaway who fit my description and ordered me to unbuckle my belt and unzip my trousers so he could check the label on my underwear. It seemed like an odd request, but I didn't know if he was a cop or not. One thing is sure: He was a pedophile. The guy began play-ing with my penis. I was scared to death. I thought my heart was going to pound right through my chest, but I was too afraid to attempt an escape. I thought he would shoot me. He sucked me for several minutes, but I was scared and my body wouldn't respond. I was afraid he wouldn't quit until I had an orgasm. But it didn't mat-ter; he obviously enjoyed it and eventually quit. I was horrified. With a cynical laugh he told me to get the hell out of there. I didn't need any persuading.

Unsettled by the trauma of this experience and unable to cope with the hardship of life on the run, I decided to return to Salyersville. It was a painful homecoming. I had accomplished nothing except branding myself as a runaway. My aunt was angry, my relatives were suspicious, and my school principal was displeased. There were chores to catch up on, excuses to be made, homework in arrears. Eventually I devised another strategy to leave. This time I decided to join the army. There was only one problem: I was fifteen. This considerable obstacle, however, was no match for my determination. I soon devised a scheme. The mother of a friend of mine was the county nurse responsible for filling out and notarizing birth certificates. My buddy acquired two blank but notarized forms and filled one out to indicate that I was seventeen. I knew I could join the army at seventeen if one of my parents signed a consent form. I could get in on my own at eighteen, but I was afraid I couldn't fool the enlistment officer. My friend Joseph Gardner was going to join me, but backed out. Nevertheless, I persevered. Knowing I wouldn't get anywhere by asking my father to cosign, I got in touch with my mother. She refused. I decided to leave anyway. Packing my few belongings, I hitchhiked toward Indiana.

The road north was my highway to freedom, or so I thought. In spite of my experience with the pedophile cop, I possessed the fearlessness born of desperation. I stuck my thumb out and mugged at passing cars. My red hair and freckled face were an asset when it came to flagging down rides. I used my hillbilly charm to get what I needed. Anytime someone picked me up, I would act as though I was starving. Some drivers gave me money, and others stopped and bought me food. I preferred cash. I was learning that a little con could get you what you needed. When I'd run away before and had to knock on doors asking for handouts, it didn't bother me. I actually enjoyed it.

The first evening out I got stranded on a lonely stretch of highway. I spent the night sleeping by the side of the road. The next day I reached Indiana and got a temporary job picking cucumbers on a pickle farm. The farmer paid me fifty cents a bushel. I could pick three or four bushels a day. Hustling on the road was more profitable and less work, but I didn't want to spend my life scamming motorists. I was determined to get in the army as quickly as possible. The news that I had run away a second time and that no one knew where I was really upset my mother. So when I contacted her again and told her I would not go back to Salyersville, she agreed to sign the consent form. She didn't really think I could get in, but I was big for my age and very self-assured. I got in with ease.

I was sworn into the army in the summer of 1958 and promptly shipped to Camp Gordon, Georgia, for basic training. It was the toughest thing I had ever done, but I was used to hardship and it didn't matter. It was the first time in my entire life that I didn't have to think about where my next meal was coming from or whether I had clean clothes or holes in my shoes. The only thing I worried about was that my true age would be discovered, a fear that haunted me every day I was in boot camp. About halfway through training, the platoon sergeant gave me a real fright. I was stretched out on the ground, resting after a forced march. The sergeant kicked the bottom of my new boots and shouted, "How old are you, soldier?" I was certain I had been found out. I jumped up and shouted back, "Seventeen, sir!" in the deepest voice I could muster. He just looked at me wordlessly for several seconds, grinned, and walked away. Fortunately I heard nothing further about it and managed to complete basic training with good evaluations and above-average scores. Not bad for a fifteen-year-old. I felt like a success. Resplendent in my army greens, I looked like one, too.

While I was in basic training I had my first real consensual sexual experience (if you don't count Imogene or the chicken). Everyone in my platoon was obsessed with women and always talking about sex. All the guys complained about the long period of enforced abstinence at boot camp. "It's been so long!" they would whine. I complained along with them, even though I was still an adolescent and had never been with a woman in my life. But this would soon change. The first weekend we had an off-base pass (and a paycheck), a group decided to head into Augusta and visit a notorious whorehouse. They took me with them. I was four or five years younger than the rest of the guys. I felt like the platoon mascot.

The whorehouse turned out to be a seedy hotel where "guests" rented rooms by the hour. Pretending as though I knew what I was doing, I checked into a room. I was all bravado and no confidence. The "bellhop" said he would send a girl right up. Well, he sent one all right, but it wasn't a girl. It was a woman. A *mature* woman. She was on the north side of forty and not particularly well preserved. Being a good little soldier, I stood up when she came in, but I was so scared my knees started shaking like a sack full of doorknobs. I couldn't stop them. I just stood there, mute and wide-eyed, while she proceeded to strip. I was frozen in place. Finally she said, "Well, get undressed! I haven't got all night!" Obediently, I did. I was embarrassed, not only because of my inexperience, but also because under my clothes I had on a pair of long underwear—a "union suit." I felt like a hick. Somehow, trembling all the while, I got my clothes off and stood there naked, wondering what to do next. She looked me up and down with the seasoned, all-knowing look of a professional. "Young man, is this your first time?" she asked. "No, of course not," I blurted out unconvincingly. "I've done it lots of times!" "Sure, honey," she replied in a tone that made it clear she didn't believe me. I never did stop shaking, but I did lose my virginity.

After boot camp I was assigned to Fort Leonard Wood, Missouri, for additional training. In spite of my age I continued to do well and enjoyed the military life. But it did not last long. Lack of education, not age, was my downfall. After I had been in the army for only seven months, word came of a general cutback in personnel. It was 1959, and the world was temporarily at peace. The Department of the Army, responding to pressure from Congress, made a decision to prune the ranks. Seniority was a criterion, and recent recruits would be the first to go. Somebody at the Pentagon decided that those with a low GET/ARI score (a general education test everyone was required to take) would get the ax immediately. I was shocked to find my name on the list of personnel to be discharged. I felt humiliated. I liked being a soldier: the strict discipline, the training, the prestige of a uniform. I couldn't stand the thought of returning to Lakeville in shame. I didn't know what to say, so I wrote to my relatives claiming to have been placed in the Army Reserve. When I was discharged, I went to Dayton, Ohio, where my mother was living.

I was only sixteen, but I was no longer a child, and it never occurred to me to resume a child's routine. I never considered going back to high school. I couldn't imagine myself in a classroom with other teenagers. I felt nothing in common with them. I was still immature, but I had the outlook of an adult. Unhappy again, I wandered Dayton's streets and took the first job I found—washing dishes at an Italian restaurant for ninety-five cents an hour. This was better than picking cucumbers but a big comedown from the army—one I couldn't stand for long. I continued to look for better employment. A couple of months later I found a job at the Dayton Mattress Factory for the grand sum of $1.15 an hour. Soon after, I moved to the United Fireworks

Company, where I made $1.35. I didn't want to be a job-jumper; I just needed to make enough money to live on. I was a teenager in an adult job market. I had no one to rely on but myself. Life-sustaining jobs were hard to come by.

The best positions in those days—at least for someone with a limited education—were at the General Motors plant, which paid big money for the time. But I couldn't get hired because of a protracted steel strike. Finally I got word that Inland Manufacturing Company, a division of GM, was hiring. I went to its employment office to sign up. There was a line of applicants a mile long. Improvising, I found a telephone, called the company, and asked for the name of the personnel director. I then went back to the employment office, all the way up to the front of the line, and told the clerk passing out applications that I wanted to see the director. I used the name I had just learned over the phone. The clerk asked why I wanted to see him. I said, "Because he called me and said I should report to work." I gave them my name, and they began to look for my application. Of course they didn't find one. Eventually they came back and told me it must have been lost in the confusion and asked me to go ahead and fill out another one. I did and was immediately put to work. I was just a kid, but I was already learning how to manipulate the system.

After I had been working at Inland for about three months, there was a union-led work slowdown. I was laid off along with many others. I couldn't bear the prospect of another demeaning job. I was tired of working under circumstances I could not control for wages so low I could hardly survive. So rather than look for a temporary position, I decided to become an entrepreneur—of sorts. I decided to invest my efforts in liquor in a market I knew very well: Lakeville. Moving in with my father, I became a bootlegger. I enlisted a high school friend to help me and began running liquor in from nearby Mount Sterling, which was in a "wet" county where liquor could be bought legally. I was underage, of course, but that didn't matter. I had no problem purchasing "legitimate" whiskey. I didn't bootleg moonshine or "white lightning," the stuff of Appalachian legend, but the so-called "government" liquor. I had an old car and circulated throughout the community making deliveries. I didn't have a driver's license, either, but this was Kentucky, and no one took any notice.

My father was one of my clients, consuming what I brought him, seldom paying, and constantly staying drunk. One day we got into a heated argument. I didn't want him drinking up all my profits. I swung a gallon jar of whiskey at him, hitting him in the face. He went down, sprawled on his back in a pool of blood. For a while I thought I had killed him, but after a few minutes he regained consciousness. He needed stitches on his face and mouth. He was too drunk to remember much about it, but the wounds on his face recorded the incident, and the red scars lingered for months. It didn't make much difference. He was never sober long enough to reflect on it. My relationship with my father was an unmitigated disaster, but my business was a success. In a short time I built a large, profitable clientele.

Unfortunately, word of my success reached the county sheriff. My uncle tipped me off that deputies were looking for me. I left my father and got out of Lakeville one step ahead of the law.

Back in Dayton I waited to be recalled by Inland while living off the savings from my bootlegging. With time on my hands, I hung out at a local bar. Lonely, I gravitated toward a girl who was a regular there. I can't remember her name. The attraction was simple: She was a beauty. For a brief moment I was in love; or, more accurately, in lust. We decided to spend the night together. When I woke up the next morning, I felt empty and disoriented. As I lay in bed, the whole weight of my miserable, lonely experience came crashing down on me. I propped myself up and looked out the window. Outside on the sidewalk I could see a uniformed sailor and his girl walking hand in hand. The sight gave me a deep sense of longing. I missed the military with its reassuring routine. I wanted to blot out the painful sense of failure I harbored from my experience in the army. I wanted to make something of myself. I got up quietly, dressed, and wrote my sleeping girlfriend a good-bye note. Returning to my room, I rooted around in my belongings, found my old, fake birth certificate, went directly to the navy recruiting station, and took the admission test. A few days later I received the news that I had passed the physical and scored in the seventy-fifth percentile on my written exam. The next day I was on a bus to the Great Lakes Naval Air Station for navy boot camp.

2.
Incapacitated by Sex

IT'S ODD WHEN YOU THINK ABOUT IT THAT A MAN *who left school after the eighth grade would own a publishing empire. Lined up in two neat rows along the left side of my desk are the thirty magazines I publish. Hustler is there, along with several other sex-oriented journals, but so are many mainstream and technical titles. My distribution company handles dozens more, including the* New York Review of Books. *The fact that I'm in this business is certainly ironic, and today, in the solitude of my office, it seems almost miraculous. I spent so many years nearly illiterate, yet now I find myself reviewing proof pages with the critical eye of a seasoned pro. I didn't attend Harvard Business School or Columbia School of Journalism. I am not a scholar or an intellectual, yet in many ways I have become a literate and savvy man. How did this happen? One thing is sure: Everything I know I learned the hard way. I am self-taught and self-made. I've made a lot of mistakes, but I've made some very good decisions, too. It seems that what I lack in formal education, I've made up for with instinct. And what formal education I did receive, I got in the navy. Looking back, I can see how the navy changed my life.*

x x x

Navy boot camp seemed easy. I was bigger, taller, and a little more mature. I had lost some of the physical awkwardness typical of boys in their early teens. But more significant was the fact that I had already survived the trials of Camp Gordon. I was still the youngest recruit in my company, but I was the only one who knew what to expect. I tackled my navy training with a vengeance. For once in my life, I had a competitive edge. I was a cocksure, aggressive kid and was quickly appointed master-at-arms for my company with an acting rank of petty officer. I always tried to work harder than anyone else and quickly compiled an outstanding record. People took notice of me. At first I relished the attention, but then my high profile began to worry me. The price of success was a loss of anonymity. I began to be afraid that someone would say, "Who is this guy?" I hadn't disclosed my previous army record, and I was worried that some routine cross-check would reveal my brief stint—and the reason for my army discharge. I wanted to succeed in the worst way, and I believed the navy offered me that opportunity. I hadn't had many breaks in my life. Consequently, my stress level rose with each succeeding day.

Finally, overcome by anxiety, I went to my commanding officer and told him the whole story. I hadn't been sleeping very well for days, and the pressure was unbearable. The CO heard me out, dismissed me, and then called in my company commander and asked him what he thought of me. As the CO later told me, my commander recommended me highly: "He's the best recruit we've had in years. The navy would be a lot better off if all of its men were like Flynt." The company commander took the whole matter under advisement, saying little. I put on a brave face for the remaining days of training, trying to suppress the gnawing feeling I had in the pit of my stomach. But my buddies could tell something was wrong. I was uncharacteristically quiet. When boot camp was complete, they went on to other assignments while I was held over for two nerve-racking weeks. My case was still being considered. Each day seemed like an eternity. I thought my whole future was at stake. Perhaps it was. Finally word came down, and the CO called me into his office. He had a look of relief on his face. He was fond of this young redheaded recruit and got right to the point: "Flynt, you can stay." I nearly collapsed as the tension drained out of my body. I stepped backward and slumped into a chair, promptly stood back up, and saluted. "Thank you, sir," I said. We chatted for a moment, and I left, feeling excited and exhausted all at once. That same day I was granted a two-week leave and returned to Dayton to celebrate.

I soon found myself pounding down beers in a Dayton bar called Little Mickey's. It was there that I met the most beautiful woman I had ever seen. Her name was

Mary. She had dark blond hair, green eyes, and a world-class body. I wanted her; in fact, I ached for her. I turned on every bit of charm I had—which I thought was considerable—but she wouldn't even let me kiss her unless we married first. I wanted to do a lot more than kiss her! I thought about it for a couple of days. In the meantime Mary flirted, said flattering things to me, and told me she wanted to settle down with a nice guy. She said I was a nice guy. I was crazy about her. In some ways I was old for my age, but in this case I exercised typical dumb-shit adolescent judgment. I agreed. "Why not?" I thought. So I told her, "Let's get married." I was thinking with my dick, a long-term trait of mine.

Mary and I went to the justice of the peace downtown and got married. It was a quickie secular ceremony that seemed painless enough at the time. In five minutes I had my ticket to nuptial bliss. That night I slept with her. It was a big disappointment. Mary was cold and dispassionate. She just lay there like a mannequin while I released a reservoir of passion that had been building up for weeks. All my pent-up stress, loneliness, and desire came pouring out of me, but it had no effect on her. My new bride didn't give anything back. Nothing. "Why?" I wondered.

I didn't find out why until later. I told my drinking buddies, "I just married a woman I met at Little Mickey's." They asked, "Who?" I said, "Mary," and described her stunning good looks in some detail. They looked on in amazement. They knew who she was. The woman had a reputation. Until we'd met, I was the only one in the place who hadn't screwed her! She was just going through the motions; she didn't care about me at all. The woman only wanted a monthly allotment check. I filed for divorce immediately.

A few days after my return to Great Lakes and my ill-fated marriage, I was sent to the Brunswick Naval Air Station in Georgia. When I was first assigned there, I was miserable. My job as a janitor was not commensurate with either my abilities or my ambitions. I hadn't joined the navy to sweep floors. Bored, I decided to divert my energy into a little scam and teamed up with a friend to sell Bibles during off-duty hours to women in the plush suburbs around the base. We found an old wheelchair that we would load into the trunk of a taxi and take to an affluent neighborhood. After unloading the chair in some out-of-sight place, my buddy got in and did his best imitation of a slobbering, contorted idiot. I would push him up to the front door of a home and ring the bell. When an unsuspecting housewife answered, my friend would laboriously attempt to speak, muttering a barely intelligible pitch about the need for her to purchase a Bible. People found it hard to watch and were always anxious to get us off their porch. After a minute or so of this painful charade I would take over, explaining that we were trying to raise money for his medical treatment. Gullible middle-class residents—men and women—would almost always make a purchase and throw in a tip, too. We sold a lot of two-dollar Bibles for ten bucks. The ruse eventually ended when someone got wise and called the police. My "handicapped" friend leaped up, tipping

the wheelchair over, and ran like an Olympic sprinter.
I was right behind him.

After my little scam ran its course, I decided to take a
more conventional route to success. I was painfully
aware that no matter how smart I was, I wasn't going
to get ahead without an education. I was nagged by an
inferiority complex, knowing I had dropped out of
school in the ninth grade and had been booted out of
the army because of my low academic scores. For some
reason I couldn't seem to let go of the embarrassment.
Every time I spoke to a college-educated officer in my
Appalachian-accented English or struggled to write
a report, I was reminded of my humble roots. Fortunately, the navy was tailor-made for someone in my
situation. I could take any number of correspondence
courses at my own pace and advance as far as my abilities would take me. There was no disapproving
teacher to look over my shoulder, no smartass kids to
compete with, no bullshit. And so I began to fill the
gaps in my general education and move on to conquer
additional, more technical material. I wanted to become a radar technician—an ambitious goal for a hick
like me.

A radar technician's job required an intimate
knowledge of electronics and math. I had grown up in
an environment where a toaster was considered high-
tech. I had never seen the inside of a transistor radio,
much less an oscilloscope. Everyone tried to discourage
me from taking the exam. But I studied like hell and
took every correspondence course that had anything

remotely to do with radar technology. I learned about the propagation of radio waves, the Doppler effect, and many other strange and wonderful things. After completing several courses, I was ready and anxious to move on. At that time the first step toward becoming a radar technician was to pass a qualifying test for "Radar Class" school. But you weren't allowed to take it without the recommendation of your chief petty officer. At first he said no, but I pestered the reluctant chief until he relented and gave me the prerequisite recommendation. He wasn't sure I could manage the exam. But I took it and passed on the first try. Everyone was surprised but me.

It was a pleasure to make the change from cleaning classrooms to studying in them. For a student, Brunswick was an interesting place. It was a center that prepared officers and noncommissioned officers (NCOs) for assignment to shipboard combat information centers, or CICs. The school was located in a series of huge buildings that housed mock-ups of the radar and communications centers of every type of ship in the navy. It was the nautical equivalent of an aviation simulator—a full-size, three-dimensional toy for grown-ups. We learned the various systems by playing with the controls, engaging in simulations, and solving problems our instructors set up for us. I loved the school and did well. After completing the course at Brunswick—I finished seventh in a class of thirty-five—the navy sent me back to Great Lakes to the "Radar A School." By this time I was on a roll. To get into that school you had to be a high school graduate, but that requirement was waived for me because I had already advanced to the rank of noncommissioned officer without a diploma. It was a boost for my self-esteem.

During the time I spent in Radar A School, the Navy Reserve ran scheduled shuttle flights between the Great Lakes Naval Air Station and Wright-Patterson Air Force Base near Dayton. Regular naval personnel could take advantage of these flights for free. I began commuting home to Dayton every Friday night and returning every Sunday afternoon. My usual hangout in Dayton was the Keewee bar, managed by my mother. A drinking buddy I met there was dating a thirty-year-old divorcée by the name of Ernestine. I got to know her, and one night she invited me to have dinner at her house and meet her daughter. The girl's name was Peggy, and she was a striking fifteen-year-old beauty. She had long black hair, alabaster skin, long eyelashes, incredible eyes, and a sensuous figure. Peggy told me she was eighteen, and I believed the lie. Like me, she was worldly-wise and seemed older than she actually was. Even if I had known she was jailbait, I would not have cared. I was dumbstruck and overcome with desire. I began seeing Peggy every weekend. Her mother accepted me right away and let me hang out at their house all I wanted—including overnight. Within a few days we were sexually involved. Unlike Mary, Peggy was a passionate and responsive lover. I was crazy about her. I thought she looked like Elizabeth Taylor, whom I had just seen in

Butterfield 8. She was the living embodiment of my seventeen-year-old fantasies.

When I finished Radar A School, the navy gave me three choices of assignment. I wanted to go to a destroyer on the West Coast, so I filled out the three blanks on my request form: "Destroyer, Destroyer, Destroyer," and added "West Coast" at the bottom. When my orders came, they read: *USS Enterprise,* an aircraft carrier based on the East Coast. I didn't get one damn thing I asked for, and in my disappointment didn't realize the assignment was an honor. My buddies were shocked: "God, how did you pull that off?" They understood what the *Enterprise* was: a brand-new nuclear-powered carrier, the most prestigious assignment in the navy. Oblivious to the significance, I told them, "I don't want it!" In fact, I protested all the way to the Pentagon. I finally reached some low-level bureaucrat by telephone. After impatiently listening to my complaint, the exasperated voice said, "Captain Depoit has handpicked this crew. You should be proud." The matter was closed. No one was willing to reassign me. In retrospect it was a good thing.

And so, in October 1962, I was assigned to the Combat Information Center aboard the spanking new *USS Enterprise,* the first nuclear-powered surface warship in the U.S. fleet. The navy gave me a short leave before we were to ship out for a three-month shakedown cruise to the Caribbean. I spent it in Dayton, taking passionate leave of Peggy. With a light heart and high hopes, I reported for duty. I was only eighteen years old and already a petty officer, second class—the youngest in the entire fleet. At an age when most boys were entering their senior year in high school, I was the equivalent of a staff sergeant in the army. This was going to be an adventure.

The *Enterprise* was the crown jewel of the fleet, and the CIC contained the most sophisticated array of electronic instruments in the history of naval warfare. I had ninety-five men under my command, most of them older than me. The CIC was the ship's nerve center and controlled the launch and recovery of all the aircraft, housed the air-traffic controllers, and contained the surface and aerial navigation systems. Everything was computerized, utilizing the first mainframe computers ever put on a ship. It was heady stuff for a kid from Lakeville.

A few weeks after I was stationed aboard ship, I had a rather extraordinary encounter. We were visited by the president of the United States, John F. Kennedy. I was assigned to duty on the bridge, serving as a liaison with the CIC. The bridge had a sweeping view, and I could see the three dark blue helicopters as they came in on final approach. The president—with an entourage of navy brass, aides, Secret Service agents, and officials—soon disembarked to greet our captain and a whole cadre of sailors in dress whites at full salute. In a moment he disappeared from my field of view, leaving the flight deck and entering a passageway below me. A few minutes later JFK stepped over the sill of the watertight door and entered the bridge. I stiffened up and stood at attention.

The captain ushered Kennedy around the perimeter of the room, explaining the various controls and systems. It was apparent that the president was going to pass within a few inches of me. He soon came so close I could smell his aftershave. He was wearing a dark blue suit and an expensive silk tie. I wanted to shake his hand but wasn't sure how to get his attention. Improvising as usual, I adjusted my stance, shifted my foot slightly, and deliberately stepped on his toe, saying, "Excuse me, sir!" I tried to make it look like an accident. The president was unfazed. Ignoring the smudge on his expensive black shoe, he looked right at me and said, "Excuse *me*," and then stopped to ask for my name and what my job was. We chatted briefly. The captain saw the whole thing and was exceedingly nervous. He stood by Kennedy's side, fearing I would say something inappropriate. Later I would think it strange that this same man's widow would help make me a financial success.

While on the *Enterprise*, I made it a point to be the best at my job. I was struggling to feel good about myself— and had reason to—but no matter how well I did, I was still haunted by feelings of failure for quitting school. My Appalachian drawl and limited vocabulary made me feel inferior. I wanted to elevate the level of my speech and eliminate all vestiges of my hillbilly syntax. It developed into an obsession. It didn't seem to matter that I had advanced faster than any of my peers. So I continued to read and take correspondence courses in the hope of building my vocabulary and academic skills. Among the courses that interested me was one called "Introduction to Electronic Counter Measures" (ECM). In it I learned the basics of monitoring enemy communications and other cutting-edge technology. I already knew a lot about radar, so ECM was a natural extension of my expertise. Having taken the course, I was qualified for further training in the use of top-secret equipment. At that time the navy had a classified school in Norfolk, Virginia, that conducted a two-month ECM course. I managed to get sent there while the *Enterprise* was in the shipyard at Newport News. It was tough and was made even more so by the fact that its curriculum and equipment were so secret you couldn't share your difficulties with anyone. Everyone there was an elite technician with a top-secret security rating. When I got back aboard the *Enterprise* and a piece of classified equipment went down, no one else on my shift could help me. Information about ECM gear was parceled out on a "need to know" basis, and the only person on my shift who "needed to know" was me. So it became a real challenge.

My new electronic expertise was put to the test soon after I returned to the *Enterprise*. As the navy's flagship aircraft carrier, we were sent to recover astronaut John Glenn from space. Our spy equipment not only could find high-flying aircraft; it could also spot space capsules—or so we hoped. We had a special piece of classified radar equipment aboard called a "height finder." At that time no one had radar that could track anything above an altitude of 60,000 feet. But the navy had built a new classified prototype radar that was first installed on the *Enterprise*. It could pick up an object at 100,000 feet or more. With the world watching and American national pride on the line, the navy wanted nothing to go wrong with Glenn's recovery. A key element in getting him safely aboard ship was the ability to detect his incoming capsule at a very high altitude. No one was sure exactly where it was going to hit the water, and we were relying on the height finder to lock on to Glenn as early as possible so his trajectory could be anticipated and charted. We wanted to get the ship within visual range quickly so our recovery helicopters could get divers in the water right away.

Three days before the scheduled splashdown, the damned radar broke. It was a complicated piece of equipment and, of course, no one had any previous experience in repairing it. The commander had everyone he could find working on it. Four technicians bent over the console for two days with no success. Time was running out. Recovery was scheduled for the next morning when I came on duty for the midnight shift. It still wasn't working. The other technicians had gone to bed. The graveyard shift was slow, and other people were minding the rest of the equipment under my supervision, so I just started dickering with the thing. In those days most electronic equipment was constructed with hundreds or thousands of hardwired connections and discrete components— none of the integrated circuits that we have now. The inside of that machine was an intimidating mass of

small-gauge, color-coded wires. The problem could
have been anywhere.

As I systematically began to check the various
connections, something happened. To this day I don't
know what. It suddenly started to work! I called the
watch commander and told him the radar was up and
running. He went and woke the captain. Everyone was
ecstatic. Since I had "repaired" the machine, they
thought I knew what I was doing and wanted me to be
the operator for the capsule's recovery. And so the next
morning I found myself in the dimly lit room, operating the machine with eight or ten officers huddled
around me. A radar scope is like a round, mono-
chrome television. A radial line sweeps around the
screen in unison with a rotating antenna outside.
Incoming objects appear as a blip on the screen, and
you can calculate their height and distance. As I stared
at the greenish display, every scan of the rotating line
heightened everyone's anxiety. I was a nervous wreck,
hoping the damn thing wouldn't break again. I didn't
want anything to go wrong for John Glenn on my
shift! And sure enough, at an indicated 110,000 feet, a
blip appeared on the screen. It worked! Everyone hoot-
ed and hollered as I tracked the capsule all the way
down to the ocean's surface. Without a doubt that was
a high point in my naval career. But not the highest.

When I look back, the best day of my naval career was
the one on which I took the General Educational
Development test, or GED, for my personal equivalen-
cy diploma. I had been studying for months and

passed it on the first try. It's hard to explain, but it was a watershed experience for me. The navy and the GED gave me the self-esteem I had always sought. The bonds of ignorance and poverty seemed broken. The whole world was opening up to me. For a kid from the hollow it was like getting a Ph.D. I was hungry for knowledge and more confident than I had ever been in my life. It was as though that exam gave me permission to explore. There was no library in Lakeville and only a tiny one in Salyersville. Up until that time I hadn't read much. But now I had a passion for books. I joined the Book-of-the-Month Club and started reading all the titles I could get. A world of possibilities opened up to my young mind. I read Napoleon Hill's *Think and Grow Rich* and Elmer Letterman's *How Showmanship Sells*. Hill's book had a great influence on me; it made my dreams seem possible. These and other books I read may seem corny now, but they opened my eyes to a world I had never seen or imagined.

In addition to books, my other passions were poker and women. I used to play cards all the time. I was making about $600 a month from my navy salary, but in some months I could double that amount with poker earnings. I had the reputation of possessing the largest slush fund on the ship. Poker paid for my luxuries and supported my habit with the girls. And it was an expensive habit. I remember one night in particular when I spent a fortune while on shore leave in France. We were anchored near Cannes. I had a pocketful of poker earnings and wanted to get off ship as quickly as possible and beat my shipmates to the best whorehouse in town. I wasn't enamored by the prospect of being the fiftieth sailor to sleep with the same whore on the same night. The radioman was usually the first one ashore, accompanied by the shore patrol. His job was to establish onshore communications before the rest of the crew was given liberty. I hitched a ride with him, wearing my shore patrol armband and carrying a nightstick. I stashed the armband and nightstick in the radio shack on the pier and headed out. No one was the wiser.

I was the first to arrive at the "hotel" with the reputation for having the best-looking girls in town. There must have been twenty women standing around in the lobby waiting for the action to start. They were all beautiful, and I couldn't decide which one I wanted. After a moment's reflection I decided, "What the hell, I'll take them all!" I said, "Ladies, come with me—*all of you!*" They looked at me like I was crazy, but I had the money in my hand, and that's all that mattered. We went upstairs to a large, ornate suite. Barking orders like a marine drill sergeant, I ordered the ladies to get undressed and line up. I walked up and down, hands behind my back, reviewing them like they were an honor guard. Then I ordered them to bend over and grab their ankles. With much giggling, they complied. I stood there for a moment taking in the sight of twenty naked French whores, ass-end up, wondering what to do next. It didn't take long to decide. I dropped my pants and started down the line, a couple of thrusts here, a couple more there, until I'd worked all the way down the row—then I went back and started again. I thought I was in heaven, but I had hell to pay later. I had so much sex that night, my back went into spasm. I was young and fit, but it didn't make any difference. I'd reached my absolute limit. I couldn't walk. My buddies—who arrived later—carried me back to the ship. It was the only time I'd been incapacitated by sex.

Two months after my night out in Cannes, the *Enterprise* docked in Norfolk, Virginia. When I got off ship, I headed straight for Dayton. My many sexual experiences at liberty ports around the world had not dampened my desire for a reunion with Peggy. However, the event that followed was not what I expected—not even in my worst nightmare.

When I arrived at Peggy's house, I was confronted at the door by her mother, Ernestine. She was in my face before I had a chance to say hello. I stepped back into the hall as she came out, shouting and gesturing wildly. Something was desperately wrong. She accused me of taking advantage of Peggy solely for my own sexual pleasure and then forcing her to have an abortion. I didn't know what she was talking about or why she was yelling at me. As I stammered, trying to get a word in, she turned around and stomped into the house, disappearing into the bathroom. I stepped forward and stood just inside the door, dazed and wondering what to do. In a moment Ernestine returned. She had something in her hand, but I couldn't tell what it was. Continuing her tirade, she thrust a jar in my face. It contained what appeared to be a human fetus preserved in alcohol. I staggered backward and tried not to vomit. She told me that if I had been more responsible, "This baby would have lived." I have no idea how she managed to obtain the gruesome specimen. I didn't know whether it was from Peggy's womb or not, although it seemed unlikely. I fled the scene, angry and confused.

Two weeks later I left the trauma of Dayton behind and sailed again with the *Enterprise*, this time to a station off Cuba and then on to a long, leisurely cruise around the Mediterranean. My routine while at sea was comprised mostly of duty time, reading, poker, and sleep. It was a comfortable and reassuring regimen. While not under way I was on shore leave in ports all over the Mediterranean. I no longer felt like a parochial Kentucky hillbilly but a man of the world. I drank it all in with a thirst born of years in isolation. I saw the sights, ate the food, drank the wine, and slept with every woman I could pay or persuade. Yet in spite of all these distractions, I missed Peggy. After the confrontation with her mother, I hadn't dared try to see her. I wrote her many passionate letters, reaffirming my love and looking forward to a future together with her. It was unusual for me to miss more than two or three days without writing. Sometimes I would write two letters a day. As the *Enterprise* cruised, every mile that passed increased the longing I felt.

When we finally docked in Norfolk again, I couldn't wait to get ashore. I took the first flight to Dayton, where Peggy met me at the airport. I was nearly overcome with emotion when I saw her. We drove straight to a motel rather than the house she shared with her mother. I felt like the happiest man alive. But it was short-lived. I hadn't noticed anything different at the airport, but when she began to get undressed, I saw that she was wearing a girdle to disguise her round, full belly. She was seven months pregnant. I hadn't seen her for thirteen months. I was shattered. I laid my head on her pregnant belly and cried. Peggy wept bitterly and begged for my forgiveness. She assured me that she had never loved anyone else. Her pregnancy, she said, was her mother's fault; the result of having been forced to go out with another man. I could see that she was miserable. I couldn't hate her for what she had done. We made love and then drove to Richmond, Virginia, and got married. It was a terrible mistake.

We set up housekeeping in Norfolk, in a small apartment near the harbor. The baby, born prematurely, spent two months in the hospital before we could bring her home. As it turned out, the teary-eyed confession of a few weeks earlier had only masked a personality incapable of truth or fidelity. Peggy had the morals of an alley cat. I soon found myself chasing sailors out of my bedroom. I was in shock. I had come home to a pregnant girlfriend—a woman I loved—married her and immediately found myself embroiled in one ugly brawl after another. Her infidelity devastated me. I nearly killed a man I caught with her. When I wasn't in a rage, I fought depression. Sure, I had screwed around in liberty ports and done a lot of things, but after I married Peggy, I tried to be faithful to her. There was no reward in it. I would never try to be faithful to any woman again.

Eventually I lost all motivation to succeed in the navy and became obsessed with the desire to get out. When my enlistment was up, I was discharged in July 1964. Following my discharge I drove Peggy and her daughter, Judy, back to Dayton. She was pregnant again. At least this child was mine. Because I was a veteran, I was able to get my old job back at Inland Manufacturing. I was soon going to have three mouths to feed in addition to my own. So I went back to work and tried to settle in. But I was restless and unhappy. My marriage was unsatisfying, and my job was much less interesting than what I had been doing in the navy. I missed the travel and the excitement of foreign shores. Working on the assembly line was mind-numbing, and there was no liberty port to look forward to. I began to wonder if I had made the right decision. I didn't want to be at Inland for the rest of my life. I couldn't imagine myself twenty years down the line, a regular lunchbox Joe, dead inside, shuffling out the factory gate and going home to a loveless marriage. I wanted to work for myself. I wanted opportunity. I wanted out. I wasn't sure exactly what I should do or where I should go, but I knew *whatever* it was, I was going to need capital. So I began to take all the overtime I could get, sometimes working two full shifts. When the first shift ended, I would crawl under one of the presses and rest until the next shift began. I took a second job working at Chrysler Airtemp across town. It kept me away from

Peggy. To cope with the demanding schedule, I began taking amphetamines.

The situation between Peggy and me continued to deteriorate. I blamed the decline on her mother. In fact, I hated her mother. Peggy was an only child, and her mother had let her screw around since she was ten years old. In some ways Ernestine acted like a pimp, always encouraging her to get involved with men. The legacy of all that bad parenting and lack of supervision was my faithless marriage with a woman incapable of fidelity. I couldn't change Peggy, and so after a few months I decided to change her mother. I don't remember how it got started, but I do remember that I had been drinking. After one too many beers I made my way to Ernestine's house, let myself in, and began to shout my displeasure. I caught her by surprise. She alternately cowered on the sofa and leaned forward, shouting back at me. I was furious, and at the height of the confrontation I threw a telephone at her, pulled a pistol out of my pocket, and screamed, "I think I'll just kill you!" Ernestine jumped up in a panic and ran past me. I pulled off a couple of rounds, shooting over her head. "You fucked up, Peggy, and now you're going to pay the price!" I screamed. In her haste to escape, she ran out the door, tripped, and fell down a flight of stairs to the street. I stomped out, leaving her in a heap on the sidewalk. I was mad as hell, but I wasn't stupid enough to actually shoot her.

My 1951 Studebaker was parked outside. I jumped in and fled, burning rubber as I pulled away. By the time I got a few blocks down the street, I was going 80. I was in a blind rage. I tried to make a left turn at Neadmore Road but couldn't bleed off enough speed. I did a four-wheel drift through some poor guy's front yard, barely missed a couple of trees, swung around the house, hit a wire fence around his just-planted garden, and blew two tires. The owners of the house were sitting on the front porch as I careened by. They scattered like flies. I just kept on going, flat tires and all, until I made it to the Keewee. I jumped out of the car, sprinted upstairs, and was pretending to shave when the police arrived. They were not fooled. I was arrested and charged with "shooting with intent to wound, drunk driving, leaving the scene of an accident, and driving with a license under revocation." Considering the fact that my car was covered with dirt and chicken wire and had two flat tires, it was hard to plead innocence. My mother's attorney, Herb Jacobs, advised me that the only way I could avoid a long prison sentence was to claim temporary insanity and submit to psychiatric incarceration. I reluctantly agreed and was sent to the Dayton State Hospital.

That state hospital was one of the worst places I had ever seen—and I had seen some godawful places. It made other facilities look like the Hilton. If you weren't crazy when you went in, you would be when they let you out. That place was a dark, filthy, foul-smelling pit. I quickly managed to get transferred to a private sanitarium. Unbelievably, it was even worse. I was put under the care of a real fossil, a ninety-year-old doctor who prescribed a regimen of electroshock therapy. It was brutal and dehumanizing. In a few days I lapsed into a state of partial amnesia. I didn't know who I was. When I left several days or weeks later, I had trouble with my memory for months. For a long time I'd meet people I knew well and could not remember their names. It was a terrible feeling. I would have been better off in a Turkish prison.

In the spring of 1965 my first daughter, Tonya, was born. It was an unfortunate time. I felt love for my child but not for her mother. The rift between Peggy and me was nearly complete. Shortly after Tonya's birth Peggy and I had another of our many arguments. She was sitting in the Studebaker, and I was standing next to the window, shouting at her. She said something to me—I can't remember what—but something snapped inside. I spit in her face. I don't understand what happened, but with that single act I stopped loving her. The release was instant. I made up my mind that I would never again be a slave to that kind of love. The day I stopped loving Peggy, my personal problems seemed to end, at least for a while. It was a turning point. Life with her had been so chaotic that it sapped all my energy; I wasn't able to channel any of it into constructive things. I cannot give her all the blame. I was emotionally immature. But it was a good thing for me to move on.

3.
Eighteen
This Week

CONSIDERING MY ROOTS, PERHAPS IT IS NOT
surprising that I got my start in the bar business. My
father was an alcoholic. My mother owned a bar.
Everyone in my family drank. My first entrepreneurial
venture was bootlegging liquor. Alcohol has played a
destructive role in my life, but ironically it also provided
me with the opportunity to succeed. It seems to me now
that the measure of my success is not what I have
achieved but rather the obstacles I have overcome. The
road to Beverly Hills is littered with liquor bottles and
pills. But as I sit here today, I am sober and clear-minded.
I don't drink much anymore; I never get drunk. I don't
smoke dope or snort coke. It's not that I am puritanical
about it. I can certainly afford to get high. You can get
any kind of drug you want in Beverly Hills. If you are
wealthy, you can get most of it by prescription: uppers,
downers, painkillers—whatever. There is no shortage of
pill-pushing doctors around here. But I don't need those
things anymore.

It was not always so. I've spent much of my life hyped-up, doped-up, or drunk. I didn't know how to control myself. If I sat down to have a drink, I couldn't stop. I'd consume the whole bottle. If I took an amphetamine to stay up and work, I'd take several more and go for days without sleeping. The fact that my father was an alcoholic is, I guess, sufficient reason to explain my former weakness for booze and drugs. But I think now that there were other reasons, too. My brother, Jimmy, says that everybody used to talk about how angry I was, that I was full of rage. Perhaps I drank to cope, to take the edge off. I guess liquor and drugs blunted my pain but sharpened my anger. But somehow, through the haze, I was single-minded and fiercely determined to succeed. I had a gift not only for the consumption of alcohol, but for the selling of it.

x x x

After breaking up with Peggy I found enough psychological space to begin thinking about something other than my miserable day-to-day existence. As I began to reevaluate my life, I remembered a passage in Napoleon Hill's *Think and Grow Rich* in which Hill argued that the energy required to be successful was the same force that went into courtship and sex. Most men, Hill maintained, spent the first half of their lives trying to impress women rather than channeling their energy into successful business ventures. This made sense to me, so I decided to direct the energy I had been investing in my dysfunctional relationship with

Peggy into some money-making venture. I did not, however, intend to give up sex. I decided rather to dispense with the romantic element of it—the emotionally risky part.

I was theoretically single now, and with a newfound enthusiasm and the added mental clarity of a less-stressful environment, I took $1,800 I had saved from my combined salaries at Inland and Airtemp and made a down payment on the Keewee bar, buying it from my mother. I agreed to pay her $6,000 and keep her on the payroll. It was early 1965. My twenty-two-year-old reasoning went something like this: I love women and I love sex. Who gets laid the most without having to make a long-term commitment? Bartenders, entertainers, and club owners. They don't have to be the most handsome or articulate; they're just around women all the time. They have the most opportunity. And so the prospect of sex and money, in combination with a low purchase price, got me into the bar business.

I bought the Keewee for a reasonable price, but it really wasn't a bargain. The place had not been doing well. It had a permit to sell beer, but no liquor license. Nevertheless, I thought I could make it into something. I had hung out in a lot of bars in my young life and thought I had a little insight into what made some succeed and others fail. It seemed to me that the key was knowing your customers and having a gimmick. The customers I knew best, of course, were working-class people like myself, especially hillbillies. There were a lot of hillbillies in Dayton, and the Keewee was located in the middle of the neighborhood where all the hicks were living. Everyone was from Kentucky, Tennessee, or West Virginia. So the first thing I did was change the name of the place to Hillbilly Haven. I decided to recast the bar's identity into a knock-down-drag-out country joint. As it turned out, it was a very good marketing decision.

The Keewee was in an old house that had been converted into a bar. The former living room was as big as a barn, and the place had a huge backyard. When I took it over, I put up horseshoe stakes out back and fenced in the yard so people could take a beer outside. I didn't know of another bar anywhere where someone could pitch horseshoes. It was a great thing in the spring and summertime. I set up a big picnic table so customers could sit, watch, and gamble on the outcome, and soon I had people coming from 150 miles away on Sundays just to play. Inside I made sure a lot of great country music was always playing, especially tunes from Hank Williams, Roy Acuff, and Johnny Cash. It was a bar where a hillbilly could feel at home. People loved it, and soon the place was full every night. The first week I sold six cases of beer; within a few months I was selling six hundred cases on Sundays alone. My rent was $150 a month, and that included my apartment upstairs! In the blink of an eye I went from making $200 a week working two jobs to more than $1,000 a week owning my own business. By the end of summer I had earned back my investment and was making more than ever. I was on my way. All this and I was barely old enough to drink legally.

I've never considered myself a violent man, but my first months in the bar business were extraordinarily bloody. If I had been catering to middle-class white-collar workers in a nice, quiet neighborhood, I wouldn't have had much trouble. But I was aiming to serve a blue-collar clientele, the kind that could drink a dozen beers in one sitting. When they got drunk, they liked to fight. These were factory workers, truck drivers, and construction workers: people who settled differences with their fists. Bar fights were a regular part of doing business, and as I soon discovered, they were something I had to deal with myself. The liquor laws in Ohio almost forced bar owners to get personally involved in any brawl that broke out in their establishments. Bars that became known as trouble spots usually didn't get their permits renewed, and the measure of that trouble was the number of calls made to the police. The price of having the cops break up a fight might have been the loss of my beer license—it was a price I wasn't willing to pay. Furthermore, if you hired a bouncer it made things worse. A burly bouncer was an invitation to every drunk who wanted to prove himself. And it was bad for business. People didn't want some burly meathead looking over their shoulders all the time. So from the very beginning I found myself breaking up two or three fights a week. These were not little tussles or shoving matches; these were knock-down-drag-out slugfests.

Ironically, the first fight I had to break up involved, among others, my mother and my brother, Jimmy. Jimmy, whom I had seen very little over the years, was a real hellion at the time. He was eighteen years old, already a heavy drinker, and on probation for a string of petty crimes. I loved him—he was my brother, after all—but he was a real pain in the ass. He considered the bar his second home and a place where he deserved special privileges—including first claim on the good-looking women. The week after Hillbilly Haven opened, Jimmy showed up with a pal named Parnell. He and Parnell immediately started hustling two women who were sitting with some other guys at the bar. The testosterone started to flow, and in a few minutes a brawl was under way. One of the men had a knife and stabbed Parnell twice. Another broke a beer bottle over the edge of the bar and cut up Jimmy with it. Somebody else threw a glass that shattered and hit my mother below the eye. The fight lasted almost half an hour. I did my best to stop it without getting hurt. If I hadn't intervened, someone would probably have been killed. The combination of fatigue and alcohol finally wore the combatants down, and I was able to break it up. The floor was covered with beer and blood; it looked like we had slaughtered a hog in there. Parnell survived; so did Jimmy. My mother had to have several stitches to close the wound on her face. That brawl was my initiation into the realities of the bar business.

Hillbilly Haven made me a single-minded person. I was willing to take just about any risk to make it a success. I didn't think much about the potential consequences of the recurring violence, even though I came close to killing a man early on. A few weeks after

Jimmy's fight I had a serious incident with a neighborhood no-good named Eugene. Eugene came from a family with a bad reputation, the worst in the area. I knew from day one that I couldn't afford to have him hanging around. He would put me out of business. I advised him to stay away, but one day he came in anyway—already drunk. I was tending bar and told him that I wouldn't serve him. Undeterred, he muttered, "I'll serve myself!" and started to come around behind the bar.

I didn't look forward to fights, but I had resigned myself to confronting the people who started them. The alternative was giving your business to the neighborhood hoodlums. Again, it was a business decision. But in this case I also felt my personal limits had been stretched too far. I do have a violent streak that can come out when people threaten me. As Eugene rounded the bar, I picked up a .38 pistol that I kept under the counter, lowered the barrel, and pointed it directly at his head. "Stop right there!" I shouted. He kept on coming. He wasn't real bright. I had already noticed that hicks had difficulty controlling their behavior when drunk, and Eugene was no exception. The asshole was not going to stop. But on the other hand I wasn't going to run. After all, it was *my* bar. As he approached I wound up and prepared to hit him as hard as I could with the barrel of the gun. His alcohol-sotted reflexes weren't too good, and he made no attempt to duck. I brought the barrel down between his eyes with a thud, and as it hit, the gun fired. The bullet split the skin on his forehead and ploughed a furrow through his scalp but did not penetrate his skull. He jolted back, then dropped to the floor. By sheer luck I hadn't killed him. I dragged him out by the ankles and deposited him in the parking lot. He never came back.

After I opened Hillbilly Haven, my day-to-day existence became one endless blur. I began working twenty-hour days bartending, managing, and promoting my new place. I was completely dedicated to the task of making money, and I was succeeding. By the end of 1965 I had bought a second bar on the east side of Dayton and named it Larry's Hangover Tavern. The Hangover Tavern was close to several factories and on a busy street. I renovated the place and put in a new jukebox, some pinball machines, and a coin-operated pool table. It was an instant success and soon was doing three times the business of Hillbilly Haven. I was bouncing back and forth between the two places, trying to keep up. Sometimes a fight would break out in one while I was working at the other. If this happened I would jump in my car, drive over like a maniac, and try to settle the dispute. Working-class bars were a high-risk, high-stress business. By now I was often working two or three days without sleep. Amphetamines kept me going. I had no personal life, least of all any involvement with a woman that included an emotional commitment. I was screwing around with several women, but it was sex, not love. I wanted to put the hurt of my relationship with Peggy behind me. Endless work and impersonal sex were my strategy. For the most part it was an effective one, but occasionally an unsolicited reminder of my past would seek me out. One such reminder was Frank Reed.

Reed was the man who had gotten Peggy pregnant. I didn't really know him, but there was no love lost between us. I had never confronted Reed because I didn't blame him for what had happened. I hated him instead for what he represented. During my marriage he was a symbol of Peggy's infidelity, and now he was a reminder of my painful past. Reed lived near the Hangover Tavern and came in one night unexpectedly. He was already stoned and cruising for trouble. It was late, and I had just emptied the coin receptacles for the pool table and juke-box. I was sorting and rolling the change as he looked around, spotted me, and approached the table where I was sitting. He paused halfway across the room, his gaze fixed on me, hands on his hips. It was a macho pose intended to impress me. The fucker thought he was John Wayne. He was a big man and bellowed, "I'm Frank Reed and I understand you think you're tough!"

A fight was inevitable. I could feel the emotion rising inside. This drunken fool was dredging up resentments I didn't want to think about. And he was threatening me in my own bar. I sure as hell wasn't going to back down. I never back down. I stood up and cradled a roll of nickels in my hand, waiting for him to get close. He walked right up to me and stopped. His face was six inches from mine. We stared at each other for a moment. Then, without blinking, I sucker punched him as hard as I could. He fell but instantly came back at me, head down like a bull. The fight was on. He knocked me over the table and down to the floor, landing on top of me. We wrestled around for a couple of minutes until somehow I ended up with my head between his knees. I was looking right up his crotch. I hit him in the balls with every ounce of adrenaline-charged energy I could muster. It was a satisfying and perverse justice. He wasn't going to be fucking anyone soon. He moaned and doubled over, gasping for breath. I jumped up and vented my rage, kicking him in the stomach, then the ribs, and finally his face. Frank Reed had become the unwitting scapegoat for all my repressed pain. I picked him up and threw him out the front door. My old memories went out with him.

With two bars making money, I decided to expand again and bought a third, this time on the west side of Dayton. Like the Hangover Tavern, it was near several factories in a working-stiff neighborhood. I decided to call it The Factory. It was close enough for people to walk to during their lunch hour, so I decided to serve food. More sales, more revenue, I reasoned, even though food wasn't nearly as profitable as liquor. By now I was beginning to understand how much you could make on what at first seemed insignificant. Those nickels and dimes that customers were putting in coin machines, for instance, were adding up to serious money. I wanted to put several more in The Factory. But that roll of nickels I'd hit Frank Read with a few weeks earlier wasn't all mine—I had to give half of it to the vending-machine company. With three bars it didn't make sense to give that money away anymore.

I could afford my own. At the Hangover Tavern the jukebox was taking in $1,000 a month; the pinball machines and pool tables were taking in another $1,200. Back then you could buy a jukebox for $1,000 and a pool table for $500. You didn't need an accounting degree to crunch the numbers. I called a vending-machine distributor in Cleveland and bought my own.

With three bars going strong, I was making four or five thousand a month on the vending machines alone. It seemed like a low-maintenance, no-brainer way to make money, so I decided to start my own vending-machine business and supply machines to other bars in town. I could undercut the competition a little and still make good money. I gave my new enterprise the immodest name of National Vending Machine Company. It sounded impressive, and people naturally assumed that it was a big outfit, even though I was running the operation out of my garage. Some of my friends thought I was crazy. The vending-machine business was reputed to be run by organized crime. Supposedly you couldn't own a machine, much less lease one to somebody else, without getting leaned on by the mob. I didn't worry, however. As people used to say in the hollow, "If you're born to drown, you ain't gonna hang." The mob had never given me any trouble. I knew many mobsters, but I'd never done any business with them. If you don't, they will leave you alone. If I was going to get hurt, it was more likely that it would be at the hands of some drunken fool. I bought cigarette, candy, and pinball machines, pool tables, and jukeboxes. I put all my innate salesmanship skills into placing them, and within a short time I had my machines in bars all over the city. When I started there were fourteen vending-machine companies in Dayton. By the end of the year I was the fourth largest.

As the months went by it seemed more and more likely that I would be killed by one of my customers. There were fights all the time. I had to cultivate a "don't fuck with me" reputation just to survive. One of those customers—a potential killer—was a tough guy named Roger Pack. Roger had been dating a woman named Mona off and on, and Mona was the owner of a bar in competition with the Hangover Tavern. Roger was a merciless, mean-spirited bar brawler. One night he and his two brothers, Earl and John, came into the Hangover Tavern. I was tending bar across town at Hillbilly Haven. The Hangover Tavern was packed—in stark contrast to Mona's. Roger and his brothers had decided to "promote" Mona's business by thinning out the crowd at my tavern. They came prepared. All three carried lead pipes, and as they walked in, they started to swing them indiscriminately, hitting people on the head and knocking them to the floor. It was mindless, brutal violence against women, old men—whoever happened to be within reach. After a few minutes of utter chaos, the hoodlums left. The bar was a bloody mess of injured, broken people, many lying in pools of blood. There were some nice folks who came in to the Hangover Tavern, good-hearted average Joes. They were beaten senseless. I was sick to my stomach when I heard about it.

I decided not to go out looking for the Packs. I was mad as hell—so mad I knew I would kill them. If I took them down on their own turf, it would look premeditated, and I'd go to jail for murder. But as it happened, I didn't have to find them. They found me. A few nights later Roger, Earl, and John sauntered into the Hangover Tavern and sat down at the bar. The unmitigated, stupid arrogance of those assholes! They had busted up my place on the previous Saturday, and they thought they could just walk in a week later as if nothing had happened. They ordered drinks in a tone that implied, "Get your ass in gear, Flynt." I thought I was going to explode, but I didn't say anything.

I knew there was going to be a fight, and I quickly collected my thoughts. There was a small plastic bucket at the waitresses' station at the end of the bar. We used it to put bottle caps in. I walked down and emptied a handful of caps into the bucket, trying to appear nonchalant. Then I picked up the bucket, leaned behind the bar, and discreetly slipped my .38 snub-nose inside. They didn't notice. They were too busy congratulating themselves on what badasses they were. With my hand on the pistol and the pistol in the bucket, I casually walked up to Earl, the one closest to me, and called his name. When he turned, I hit him square in the face with the gun. I hit him so hard the trigger guard bent and crushed my finger, pinching a chunk of flesh out of it. I didn't notice the pain. Earl sat stunned and glassy-eyed, blood trickling down his nose. I hit him a second time. John and Roger jumped up and started for me. I pointed the pistol at them and

[61]

shouted, "Sit down, you motherfuckers, or I'll blow your heads off!" They slowly sank to their seats. I hit Earl a third time. And a fourth. He was still sitting upright on the stool, blank-faced, his reptilian brain unable to respond. He was a mute, motionless, easy target. He was also a worthless piece of shit and deserved every blow. I hit him one more time and gave him a little shove with the end of the barrel. He fell backward to the floor. "Get the fuck out of here and take him with you!" I shouted to his brothers. "If I ever see you in here again, I'll kill you." After they left, I noticed my bleeding finger was still stuck in the guard. I couldn't have pulled the trigger if I had wanted to.

My run-in with the Pack brothers was a watershed for me. You had to treat hoodlums with a firm hand if you wanted to stay in the bar business. But the violence was wearing me down. I'd had too many close calls. I decided to upgrade my business and appeal to a higher class of people. My first experiment in an upscale establishment was my fourth place, a bar I bought on north Main Street and named Whatever's Right.

Whatever's Right was the first club I owned that featured hostesses who danced. I screened dozens of women and hired twelve of the best looking. I wanted them to be the centerpiece of a posh cocktail lounge, an elegant little place with a good sound system and popular music. There were a lot of guys who liked to go to a club and grind a girl on the dance floor. I wanted a mix of good dance tunes from fast rock 'n' roll to slow, sexy stuff. The whole idea was to appeal to lonely men, middle-aged and up, in a controlled environment.

I set strict policies for the hostesses. The first rule was, "Never ask a man to buy you a drink, but never turn one down." I instructed the barmaids to pour the hostesses' drinks short so they didn't have to worry about getting drunk. The second rule was, "Ask the guy to dance." The scenario I envisioned was this: A guy walks in, sits down, orders a drink, and gets it; the hostess returns a little later and asks, "Excuse me, sir, but could I have this dance?" I thought it would blow guys away. It did.

The club became a huge success. It was such a success, in fact, that several copycat bars were soon in competition with me. I wanted to stay a step ahead of them. It was early 1968. For some time I had been tracking the success of a new phenomenon called "go-go" clubs. They had started in California, and spread to Phoenix, Tucson, and then Houston. But there were no go-go clubs in the East. I thought that one might be a smashing success in Dayton, but I had never actually seen a go-go club in operation. So I decided to go to Phoenix and check one out. I went to a place called the Hi-Liter Club. To say the least, I was impressed. The club featured a bevy of good-looking dancers dressed in minuscule bikinis, gyrating to the latest music. I loved it so much that I offered one of the girls $100 if she'd take off her bikini on the spot and give it to me. She did. I returned to Dayton with the little gold lamé souvenir, determined to start my own go-go club.

My instincts told me that the club should be located in downtown Dayton. Conventional wisdom at the time considered downtown a bad choice. Inner cities in the East were being deserted, and their central cores were disintegrating. Nevertheless, it seemed right to me. I went with my intuition. After some looking around I found an old greasy spoon for sale. It was a godawful place: an eighty-year-old dive with a liquor license. I paid $15,000 for it, the license and all. It needed work but it had potential. Inside was an old hand-carved wooden bar right out of the Roaring Twenties with fluted columns on the sides, a big ornate top, and a huge mirror cracked in four places, as if it had been shot. The bar would make a good centerpiece, I decided, but the rest of the place was beyond hope. The plaster on the ceiling was cracked and sagging. The old wood lath was showing in a few places. I didn't want to spend the money to install a drop ceiling, and so I decided to paint it flat black; after I did, the ceiling just disappeared. I patched some holes, painted the walls, and bought some cheap paintings—nudes on black velvet. Then I put down red carpeting, built a little stage, and brought in cocktail tables. I ended up spending only about $5,000.

I kept the place open during remodeling so the existing customers—mostly winos and drunks—could come in and spend money. One day I was sitting at the bar next to an old hooker, thinking out loud. I couldn't decide what to name my newest club. She looked at me and said, "Hey, honey, why don't you name it after my old money-maker?" and slapped herself on the ass. "Good idea," I thought to myself. "I'll call it The Hooker." I sat there for a minute, satisfied with myself, and then thought, "Wait a minute. I'm gonna call it the Hustler Club." The name stuck. With the theme established, a couple of days later I hung the framed pictures of several famous mobsters over the bar. I called them the Hustler Club Board of Directors. A friend of mine, a cop on Dayton's vice squad, was sitting at the bar after hours one night. I said to him, "The bar looks authentic, but the pictures lack something." Not saying a word, he took out his pistol and shot a hole through one of the portraits. "Is that better?" We looked at each other for an instant; then I took out my pistol, too. We emptied them into the other pictures. Glass flew everywhere. When we were done, it looked right. Customers would always ask, "How'd those bullet holes get there?" I wouldn't answer. I'd just look at them and smile. I had reason to smile. I cleared a $5,000 profit the first week the Hustler Club was open.

Shortly after I opened the Hustler Club, I got a call from my bank in Dayton. I had borrowed a little money to do the remodeling, and the bank wanted me to repay it. We had a disagreement about whether the note was due. The guy on the phone annoyed me. I thought he was arrogant, but more important, I thought he was wrong. By the time I hung up, I was really pissed. I had the money. It wasn't that I couldn't pay; it was the principle of the thing. In a flash of inspiration I decided to pay off the bank and get some publicity for the club at the same time. I had an employee go out to the local discount stores and purchase twenty wheelbarrows. At the same time, several other employees were making the rounds to different banks all over town, buying rolls of pennies—enough to pay off the whole debt. They brought them back to the Hustler Club, and I had my go-go girls unwrap the pennies and put them in the wheelbarrows. The next day I led a procession along the sidewalks of downtown Dayton to the bank. The go-go girls, in costume, pushed the wheelbarrows through the front doors into the lobby and dumped the pennies on the floor. The *Dayton Daily News* sent a photographer. The story was picked up by the wire service, and the next day pictures of the girls were in papers all over the country. The bank took it in good spirits, although it did strain its dignity a little.

In the summer of 1968, with the Hustler Club and Whatever's Right going strong, I sold Hillbilly Haven and Larry's Hangover Tavern. I was spending time trying to develop National Vending Machine Company and wanted to expand my "upscale" bar business. I said good-bye to the two humble places that had given me my start. I wasn't sentimental about it. Immediately I bought another property in the heart of the city and decided to open a new, exclusive club. I wanted to call it Talk of the Town. It would be the first club in Dayton with runway stages, expensive chandeliers, flocked velvet wallpaper, and plush toilets. I wanted to book an unusual act for the opening and remembered a go-go girl I had seen on my trip to Phoenix. Her name was Tammy Tyler, a slender, long-legged blonde who had an unusual, attention-getting act. She danced on the ceiling, using a contraption similar to gymnastic rings. She could hang upside down and dance for four or five minutes. It was pretty amazing. I managed to sign her for a two-month contract to come to Dayton and open the club.

Talk of the Town opened in October 1968, right on schedule. It was the first club that I had built from scratch. It reflected my ideas of what a first-class place should be. The opening party was scheduled for nine o'clock Friday night, and the carpet layers finished at eight. No sense being early. I had invited about five hundred friends, business acquaintances, and others. By nine we had a big crowd. I stood up on the new runway to make a brief statement that turned into an emotional speech. I found myself telling the crowd how I had grown up poor in Kentucky, started in the bar business with $1,800, and worked hard until I could build this club. I started to tear up, got embarrassed, told the soundman to cue up the music, and brought out Tammy Tyler. All eyes in the mostly male audience shifted in her direction. I stepped down into the crowd and started circulating, greeting people with handshakes and backslaps. It was a grand moment.

According to the experts the first Hustler Club should have failed. Ralph Slyder, an old-time beer distributor in Dayton, told me I was crazy when I decided to carry only two labels and charge high prices for them. He didn't understand how I could hire so many hostesses, either. "Too much overhead," he opined. I knew he was wrong. "I'm selling pussy by the glass," I used to say, "and my customers don't care about the price of drinks." I knew what I was doing, and I made my own rules. I never let hookers in the club and only hired wholesome-looking girls. I wanted to serve the solitary businessman who would otherwise be sitting in a hotel room, staring at four walls and watching Johnny Carson. They were lonely. They wanted a woman, and if she was pretty, all the better! I carefully instructed my hostesses to pay special attention to the guy who was getting a little older and fatter, the one who smelled of cigar smoke. No girl would look twice at him in another club. This kind of guy had money, maybe even an expense account. I told the girls that, when talking to a customer, they must never complain and absolutely never nag. These guys got enough at home. Chances were, they had a wife who dressed sloppily, had bad manners, and had a stinky pussy. I was as blunt as that. It worked.

Gradually I developed what amounted to an indoctrination program. I ran a tight ship. There was more hanky-panky in a church pew than in my clubs. I only sold the *hope* of hanky-panky. I developed a program that seemed like a combination of the Naval Academy's honor code, the rules of conduct for a nunnery, and the regulations for the Miss America Pageant. I lectured the girls on how to handle amorous customers, ward off pimps, behave like ladies, and not offend customers. I admonished them to tell the truth about their work, never complain about the club, and not discuss their personal lives or other girls. They weren't allowed to accept tips, eat in the club, sit with each other, or discuss their pay. I instructed them to clap for other girls after each dance, help the waitresses clear tables if they got behind, and take their jobs seriously. I paid them different amounts, depending on their personality, appearance, adaptability, and professional ability—in that order. I had each hostess read and sign a list of nineteen club rules. For all of this I compensated them well.

Most of the girls earned between $150 and $300 a week—very good money in those days. Hundreds of girls applied to be hostesses. I advertised the jobs in the newspaper, always referring to go-go dancing as a profession, like that of an airline hostess. Applicants were treated to a slide presentation and tape commentary that covered everything from deodorants to how to introduce yourself to customers. The best applicants always appreciated the professionalism of my approach. I attracted a lot of well-educated, pretty, and talented young women. Those who made the cut danced on a spotlighted pedestal for exactly six minutes. When they were done, they came down, got dressed, and mingled with the patrons.

With my formula set, I opened a whole string of Hustler Clubs across Ohio from 1968 to 1971. Expanding out of Dayton, I moved into Cincinnati, Columbus, Cleveland, Toledo, and Akron. I was going at a furious pace, never stopping. I had been using amphetamines since 1964, and they had become a regular part of my regimen. The little "black beauties" kept me going day and night. By this time, four days without sleep was not unusual. I was wheeling and dealing, driving a big Lincoln, wearing flashy clothes, and tipping like a millionaire. I would frequently yell at my friends, "Goddammit, stop dragging your feet!" Those little pills drove me to excess in every part of my life, including sex. They had an extraordinary effect on my sexual appetite—something that needed no stimulation in the first place. During that period I had a number of ongoing relationships and countless one-night stands. I was insatiable, sometimes having a different woman every four or five hours. There may have been someone who had more women than I did, but I seriously doubt it. It got to the point where I couldn't remember who I'd screwed. I'd have to ask Jimmy or someone, "Have I fucked her yet?" I'm not as blunt now. I usually say, "I played the field pretty heavily back then." It's a deliberate understatement. I remember my secretary saying to me once, "That's eighteen this week—and it's only Friday." I said, "Huh?" She said, "You know what I mean. If they've been in your office more than ten minutes, you've fucked 'em." I couldn't argue. The more I got, the more I wanted. Sex was like a drug.

During this period I had three ongoing relationships, all of which produced children, and one of which resulted in a brief marriage. The first was a beauty named Amanda Carson. She was a country girl, a young widow whose husband had been killed when their house trailer caught on fire. Her story was a poor-white-trash soap opera. I liked her, but her countrified pace and domestic taste were in conflict with my own. Our stormy relationship, which lasted for several months, produced a child, my daughter Lisa. The second serious involvement was with Kathy Barr, a woman I met when she applied for a job at the first Hustler Club. She was a tall, gorgeous blonde in her mid-twenties. Kathy was divorced and had three kids. I had originally seen her dancing at another club, the Dragon Lady, in 1967. Kathy was probably the best sexual partner I ever had. We dated on and off for about eighteen months, and she became pregnant. In late 1968 I married her, and she gave birth to our daughter, Theresa—just after we broke up. After many intervening relationships I met Flora (Sam) Griffith. She was a barmaid at the Columbus Hustler Club. Sam was a pretty brunette and a very good person. I began an on-again, off-again affair with her. We lived together briefly, and she, too, got pregnant. Sam was as promiscuous as I was, so I wasn't sure at first if it was my child. But after the boy was born, it was obvious: He was mine. We named him Larry, Jr. I loved my children and supported them well, but I simply could not commit myself to one woman. I don't think men were meant to be monogamous.

The juggernaut seemed as though it would never stop. By early 1973 I had eight Hustler Clubs, with three hundred people on my payroll. I was well on my way to making a million bucks a year. My least successful club was clearing $75,000 annually and the best nearly $100,000. I was commuting around Ohio from club to club in a chauffeur-driven limousine, part of a whole fleet of limos I had purchased. When I opened the eighth club, I started giving out memberships. They were part of a promotional scheme I'd devised, primarily for traveling businessmen, that included a plastic card entitling the bearer to a discount on drinks and free limousine service from their hotels. With a membership mailing list steadily growing, sometime in 1972 I started to think about a newsletter that would introduce new dancers and let members know if their favorite girl had moved to a different club. Many of my clients traveled throughout the state, patronizing Hustler Clubs in every city. But in the midst of all the growth and hoopla, trouble was brewing.

My vending-machine business was starting to be a money loser. At one time I had hoped to list my National Vending Machine Company as a public corporation on some stock exchange. It was not to be. I made a couple of mistakes and seriously underestimated the amount of capital required to make it go. Probably the worst mistake I made was the purchase of a jukebox franchise. I had come across some literature about a new German-made jukebox housed in a wooden cabinet with flocked felt panels in "designer" colors. I thought it had great market potential because its classy, low-key looks would attract clients who did not want a gaudy American-style chrome and glass model. I bought the exclusive Ohio franchise from a West Coast firm and immediately set out to find a large client. I decided that the Holiday Inns were a good prospect. The president of the chain was a man named Kimmons Wilson. Wilson had recently been on the cover of *Time* and *Life* magazines, and the Holiday Inn was a growing, successful chain. Wilson was headquartered in Memphis, Tennessee. I loaded up a couple of the German jukeboxes and headed out to see him with two of my employees.

Of course I didn't have an appointment, nor had I ever met the man before. I never let such details slow me down! When we got to Memphis, we checked into the Holiday Inn and wrestled the two machines up to our room. I went to the executive offices in the headquarters building nearby and asked to see Wilson. I was a nobody without an appointment, and Wilson was protected by a whole phalanx of receptionists and secretaries. I worked my way from one to the other until I got to his private secretary. She turned me down flat. I walked out into the hallway, got a drink of water, took a deep breath, turned around, and marched right past her into Wilson's private office. I extended my hand to the startled executive, introduced myself, and started talking. The indignant secretary followed me in but was shooed away by Wilson. I guess he admired my chutzpah. We hit it off, and forty-five minutes later we were walking over to look at my machines.

Wilson was impressed by the jukebox and asked whether I could supply other kinds of vending machines in similar cabinets. We discussed the factory in Germany, service requirements, and a lot of other details. It was obvious that a sale was imminent. Wilson said he would discuss my proposal with his board and prepared to go back to his office. As he left, he turned around and said, "Everyone who works with this company is required to have a high moral character and an impeccable reputation. Would you send me a personal history and résumé?" Oops. When I got back to Dayton, I pulled together a résumé and mailed it to Memphis. I wasn't optimistic. A few weeks later I received a letter turning down my proposal. A deal with the Holiday Inns would have put the company on a solid footing. As it was, I had to continue building the business one bar at a time. It was a tough go. The other large vending-machine companies made a practice of lending money to bars and other places in exchange for an installment contract. They would put their machines into the location and then keep all of the money they produced until the loan was paid off. Hundreds of small businesses would use these loans to renovate their establishments or get started in a new location. I didn't have enough capital to compete with them.

As I got further and further into the vending-machine business, I got more and more in debt. I began to siphon funds out of the Hustler Clubs to support it. The expensive German jukeboxes were breaking my back. I was importing the complicated machines directly and had to put up substantial money in advance. Furthermore, I had to get involved in service and stocking spare parts. I did manage to place a lot of machines, but even this eventually worked to my disadvantage. As word of the German machine's popularity in the higher-class lounges spread, the big American manufacturers such as

Seeburg and Wurlitzer began manufacturing their own competing models. I was feeling the pressure and made some unwise decisions. Eventually National Vending Machine went under. It was threatening to take the Hustler Clubs with it. I had to do something to raise cash and get back on track.

4.
From Raunch
to Riches

I NEVER SAW IT COMING: THE ANGER, THE DISGUST, *the moral outrage. From the outset* Hustler *made people uncomfortable and at times apoplectic. Without a doubt* Hustler *is the most reviled of the mass-circulation porn magazines, and I have been the most hated of publishers. One man was so angry he shot me. This is a repressed nation, especially the middle class. My readers divide into two groups: the lower social classes and the highly educated. It's the people in the middle, the vast bourgeois masses, who truly despise me. I violate their middle-class sensibilities and trample on their sexual aesthetics. Working-class folks, for the most part, prefer the unromanticized body of* Hustler *to the soft-focus, idealized women of* Playboy *and* Penthouse. *I give them what they want. I used to say that I'd rather have ten truck drivers than one college professor reading* Hustler. *That's the market I went after. But I captured another one, too. When I could afford my first demographic study, I found out that* Hustler *had a bigger percentage of highly edu-*

cated readers than either Playboy *or* Penthouse. *People who are highly educated—the ones with Ph.D.s and graduate degrees—are less hung up on conventional morality. When I spoke at Harvard a few years ago, a professor told me that* Hustler *reminded him of the old ribald classics. He and other academics are fascinated by the way people respond to the content of my magazine. So am I. I think it says a lot about our culture.*

As I sit here today thinking about my roots, I can see how my hillbilly disgust with anything pretentious or phony has generated both anger and success. Hustler *became a success because I was willing to bypass the sexual hypocrisy of my competitors and cater to the erotic imaginations of real people. I have railed against the institutions and people who have held down the common, ordinary citizen: government, the rich, organized religion. In the pages of* Hustler *I have satirized and ridiculed every institution that exercises illegitimate and corrupt power. I have dared to portray people's real sexual fantasies, not those that conform to someone else's idea of what is appropriate. Little did I guess, when I took my first unsure steps into the publishing business, that all this would happen. I just followed my instincts. Those instincts brought me to this office.*

x x x

Bachelor's Beat was a little rag I had first noticed near the entrance to the Hi-Liter Club in Phoenix, when I'd gone west to check out a go-go bar. It had piqued my interest in publishing. The *Beat* was a local entertainment newspaper that carried nightclub and theater news plus features on health, love, sex, marriage, and the idiosyncrasies of people. I liked its straightforward copy and unpretentious tone. It seemed to me that a similar tabloid-format publication could be a success in Dayton and a good adjunct to my bar and vending-machine businesses. Before I left Phoenix, I decided to check it out. I called a cab and went over to the address on the masthead. Unlike the corporate headquarters of the Holiday Inns, the offices of *Bachelor's Beat* were small and unguarded. There were no secretaries with the polite-but-firm demeanor of bull terriers. I strolled into the office unopposed and introduced myself. The publisher's name was Jerry Evenson. I said I was a nightclub owner from Dayton, pulled a wad of bills from my pocket, and said, "I appreciate your paper, and I'd like a subscription."

Evenson assumed a beatific smile and looked at me as though I were an angel. He had just been talking to an associate, Boye De Mente, about his desire to franchise the *Beat* nationally. And here I was, his first prospect—unsolicited—standing across from him with a pocketful of cash. I must have seemed like a gift from heaven. He gave me his pitch, told me a franchise for Dayton was available, leaned back in his chair, and waited for my response. "I'll take it," I said without a moment's hesitation. I picked up the phone on Evenson's desk, dialed Dayton, and had $5,000 wired as a partial down payment. I didn't know a damn thing about publishing, of course, so Evenson agreed to help me with the logistics. Before I left, we worked out a plan in which I would send raw copy to Phoenix, and Evenson's staff would edit it, combine it with other articles, and send back to me—via air freight—a complete set of negatives, ready to make plates and go to press. When I got home, I made arrangements to have the tabloid printed in Cincinnati.

For a few weeks everything went smoothly for my Ohio franchise of *Bachelor's Beat*. But about two months after I bought it, Evenson's Phoenix offices were padlocked by the IRS for nonpayment of withholding taxes. This left me in a real bind. Without the support of a home office I had to produce the whole paper myself. My short apprenticeship had come to an abrupt end. I hastily assembled my small staff, brought in a former employee of Evenson's, and conducted a quick course in newspaper publishing. What we lacked in sophistication we made up for in enthusiasm. I was twenty-seven years old and didn't believe I could fail. I had been distributing the *Beat* for free at nightclubs, bars, restaurants, and hotels. People were picking it up and reading it, and I was beginning to attract some advertising. It seemed to me that the best way to increase circulation and revenue, and to build on the foundation I had already established, was to put the *Beat* out on the street along with the mainstream newspapers.

So rather than retreat or succumb to the anxieties of being on my own, I went out and bought ninety-six coin-operated newsracks and proceeded to expand the circulation of *Bachelor's Beat* in Dayton. Within days after receiving delivery of the racks, I had applied for a permit to distribute them all over the city. Much to my surprise, it caused a minor furor. The political establishment in Dayton was ultraconservative and considered the *Beat* a plague on the city. They insisted that the presence of the newspaper would weaken the moral fiber of the community and increase crime. I didn't know at the time that it was the same kind of false moralism and political bullshit I would face in the years to come. I finally got my permit, but only after much wrangling. Someone finally remembered that the First Amendment applied to me, too. But the pressure continued, both from the authorities and from vandals who frequently broke the racks and sometimes stole them.

I ran *Bachelor's Beat* for about two years, always managing to keep it alive, but never making a profit. When my vending-machine business went belly-up, I decided to sell it. I was at a low point, fiscally and emotionally. I needed to replace some of the cash I had siphoned out of the clubs to support National Vending, and I wanted to get out of Dayton. I put the *Beat* up for sale, asking $75,000. No one was interested. After weeks of searching for a buyer, I finally ended up selling it to the son of the man who owned the shop where it was printed. I got the grand sum of $4,000. At that point I didn't much care; I just wanted out. The *Beat* didn't make me any money, but it provided my first taste of publishing.

The financial fiasco of the National Vending Machine Company, its eventual failure, and the sale of *Bachelor's*

Beat narrowed the range of my activities considerably and allowed me to focus solely on the success of the Hustler Clubs. Without the cash and time drain of my vending-machine business, the pressure on the clubs was relieved. I was still in debt, but it was now an amount that seemed fixed and manageable. So I set about the task of promoting the clubs and paying off my creditors with a new burst of energy. At the center of my promotional strategy was the Hustler Club membership program, and as part of that program I decided to send a monthly newsletter to members. In March 1972 I mailed our first edition out. The masthead read: *Hustler Newsletter*. It was an innocuous-looking black-and-white, single-fold, four-page bulletin with short articles on some of the go-go dancers and a couple of feature stories. It wasn't much, but it was a start. The April edition looked about the same. Nevertheless, the newsletter was surprisingly well received. I got several calls from customers urging me to continue the newsletter and expand it. I took their advice. In May I switched to an eight-page format and shortened the name to *Hustler*. Two months later I went to sixteen pages and two colors. In February 1973 I expanded to twenty-four pages, and in August to thirty-two. The little newsletter had grown into a small magazine.

In early 1973 it looked as though I would recover financially. Club memberships were proliferating, and the newsletter was doing well. It seemed for a moment that—finally free of the liabilities of my now-defunct vending-machine business—I would be able to enjoy the profits from my clubs. I had stopped using amphetamines and wasn't drinking so much. For the first time in years my head was clear, and the future seemed bright again. I had taken the steps necessary to resolve my cash position and get back on track. But then something happened that I never could have anticipated. In mid-1973 the Arab oil embargo was imposed, and the gloom-and-doom crowd began to predict that the industrialized world would never be the same. Businessmen everywhere became fiscal conservatives overnight. Within a few months the country was in a recession. The Hustler Clubs were highly dependent on out-of-town businessmen with expense accounts and discretionary income. My revenues plummeted as companies sharply curtailed travel and cut back on frills. My road to recovery now became a highway to hell. Instead of retiring my debts, I was taking out loans. As the situation continued to deteriorate and my cash flow turned into a trickle, a flood of notes, bills, and taxes became due. My optimism turned to panic as I kept up a frantic pace. But nothing I did seemed to help. When the pressure got to be more than I could bear, I'd say, "I gotta go fuck somebody!" I would leave, find my current girlfriend—or a new one—burn off the pressure with an hour of furious sex, come back refreshed, and return to work.

One possibility for making money, I thought, was to expand my little club magazine into a national publication. I wanted to raise cash by trying to sell franchises for additional Hustler Clubs, and a national magazine would be a good source of advertising. I was beginning to think that a market niche existed for a new men's publication—a niche that no one was exploiting. When I published *Bachelor's Beat*, I had come across a distribution company named Kable News in New York. I decided to go see them and try out my idea. The president wouldn't give me the time of day, so I ended up seeing the executive vice-president, a guy named Paul Hendershot. With much persistence, I got in to see him. I showed Hendershot my little two-color magazine. I knew it needed further development—it would have to be thicker and produced in full color—and said so. But Hendershot could barely hide his pessimism for my prospects. He told me to go back to minding my clubs. As we spoke, a man walked by the open door behind me. Hendershot said, "Ron Fenton is here. He publishes *Gallery*, a kind of workingman's *Esquire*. Why don't you speak to him? He can tell you the realities involved."

Fenton, as it turned out, was a friendly man. We chatted for a few minutes and discovered that we were staying at adjacent hotels. He said he would call me later in the day. After I got back to my room, he did call, and we met later that evening in the bar of the New York Hilton. Fenton, I learned, was in a financial bind. No wonder he was friendly. He proposed that, instead of trying to upgrade my own publication into a national magazine, I could buy a piece of *Gallery* instead. His magazine had a circulation of over one million. He offered to sell me a 10 percent interest in exchange for a loan of $50,000 and an exchange of stock. I would give him 10 percent of Mini-Clubs of America (my holding company) and receive 10 percent of *Gallery*'s stock. I was already putting out $5,000 a month to print and distribute *Hustler* to club members. It didn't seem like much of a risk. I agreed, and we worked out the details before I returned to Ohio. The last edition of the *Hustler* newsletter, "The Official Publication of Mini-Clubs of America," was set for October 1973.

On November 1, 1973, I merged my little magazine with *Gallery* and became its copublisher. An announcement in the front of the edition declared it to be the "new official publication of the Hustler Clubs." I made the first of five scheduled $10,000 payments, and we were off and running. Fenton and I published three joint issues before our little venture came screeching to a halt. Kable News, the magazine's distributor, decided they had advanced more money than they could expect to get back and exercised an option in their distribution contract to foreclose on the magazine. Already stressed out, I had another fiasco on my hands. Kable News had no faith in me, a young upstart, and had thrown out Fenton, the old pro. There was no way to go on. I was even deeper in debt now, and Fenton was out of a job.

A short time later, in May 1974, Fenton called me with a proposal. He wanted to start a new men's magazine from scratch and distribute it through a small company called Capital Distributing in Derby, Connecticut. I was interested. Although I had virtually no money, I offered to finance the venture. What I had was cash flow, and I could either use it to chip away at my debts—for the rest of my natural life—or risk it on a new venture that held out the possibility of making a complete recovery. It was an easy choice. The fact that I knew next to nothing about publishing a national magazine didn't faze me. I've never been risk-aversive. I was at an age and place where I could be motivated to do something by the sheer impossibility of the challenge. My friends told me I was crazy to even think about it. Their pessimism only made it seem more interesting. So with a combination of world-class naiveté and my usually reliable instincts, I made a date to meet with Capital Distributing. Fenton would provide the credibility, and I would provide the cash.

Before I met with Capital, I decided to do a little research. I had never really read men's magazines before. I might have seen one copy of *Playboy* in my life, and I had never seen *Penthouse*. I had so much sex, wherever and whenever I wanted it, that I had never sought the solace of men's magazines. Lonely guys, I supposed, read them with one hand. I didn't need to; I had the real thing. So I went to a newsstand and bought copies of *Playboy* and *Penthouse*, took them home, and studied them. The first thing that struck me was the editorial content. It wasn't much different, if at all, from what you could find in mainstream magazines. I quickly concluded that the text didn't make a damn bit of difference. The pictures were responsible for the sales. But in sizing up the photos, it seemed to me that something was missing.

Both publications made the implicit assumption that men are turned on by women with big breasts, great butts, nice legs, and perfect faces. As far as it goes, I thought, that's true. But the men I knew, working-class guys, were turned on the most by female genitalia. That was certainly true for me. I felt that if someone published a magazine more attuned to what the average Joe really liked, a whole new market could be created. To put it bluntly, if you got the models to spread their legs a little wider, you'd sell more magazines. I made a mental note of this.

Capital Distributing wasn't exactly a giant in the business. It handled titles like *Country Song Roundup*, *Hit Parade*, and a few comic books. But they were aggressive and on the lookout for a magazine with mass appeal. Capital had contacted Fenton when *Gallery* went belly-up and encouraged him to start a new publication. Fenton said he had no money but knew someone who did—me. Fenton and I went to Derby and were greeted by Capital's vice-president, Ron Scott. I told Scott that I was ready to invest in a national men's magazine, and he said, "Fine! Fenton has it, and it's going to be called *Pleasure*." "I'd like to see it called *Hustler*," I replied. Scott didn't like the name. He thought it had bad connotations and said, "You know, it sounds like somebody 'hustling' somebody else, or maybe a magazine about hookers." We argued for a while. Scott kept holding out for the name *Pleasure*, and I kept insisting on *Hustler*. Finally I stood up, looked at him across the desk, and said, "If it's named *Hustler*, I'll put up the money. If it's

Pleasure, good-bye!" He caved in. "Okay, okay."

After we decided on the name, we got down to business. To get the magazine going I was going to have to raise enough money to front the first six issues. I wouldn't see a dime from Capital, I was told, until the seventh issue. It was going to take about $500,000 to get started. "Five hundred thousand!" I thought to myself. "How the hell am I going to raise that much money?" On the way back to Ohio I figured it out. I would stop paying withholding tax for my employees and sales tax to the state. I estimated that I could quickly come up with about $350,000 by diverting the tax money and raise the rest by various other means. So that is what I did. I don't advise people to use this as a means of raising venture capital. As my attorney later told me, "You know, if they had caught you, they could have put you *under* the jail, not in it!"

Volume 1, number 1, of the new *Hustler* came off the presses in July 1974. The masthead listed me as the publisher, Ron Fenton as copublisher, and my brother Jimmy as vice-president. It was hastily assembled in Chicago and looked like a high school version of *Playboy* with a little *Penthouse* thrown in. In my first publisher's statement I wrote, "Anybody can be a playboy and have a penthouse, but it takes a man to be a hustler." Maybe so, but the magazine was a fucking disaster. It looked terrible. I had included in my agreement with Fenton a clause that allowed him time to decide whether he wanted to stick it out before he became a vested stockholder. When he saw the magazine and what a mess it was, he opted out. With two weeks to assemble the second edition, I moved the offices to Columbus, Ohio, and with no knowledge of the national magazine business, proceeded, in a panic, to get it together. I hired some Ohio State University students to freelance articles, bought some stock photos from Graphics House in New York, and slammed together the August issue. I bought the rights to the cover photo from a photographer I knew. I had seen the picture hanging on his wall. We got the issue out, but it looked awful.

The next issue wasn't much better, but I was finally succeeding in giving the magazine a little personality. I wanted it to reflect my own frankness and irreverence. The photos in issue number 4 were a little more explicit and featured models with their pubic hair exposed—and one with her pubes dyed red, white, and blue. It was patriotic porn. But not everyone was impressed. By this time we had gotten our first review, in the New York sex tabloid *Screw*. In a column written by Bruce David, *Hustler* was lauded for edging out *Refrigerator Monthly* as the most boring magazine in America. I called Al Goldstein, *Screw*'s publisher, and told him that David's description was apt. Then I returned the favor by hiring David. He's worked for me ever since. It was a good long-term decision. Bruce David proved smart, savvy, and able not only to understand my vision but to implement it—bringing top-flight writers and editors into the pages of *Hustler*.

The first models for *Hustler* came from my own nightclubs. After the third issue I began placing small ads in the classified sections of newspapers all over the state. I got an amazing response from women who were eager to pose nude. As I was to find out, it was easier getting models in Ohio than in Los Angeles. At first I paid models $500 per layout. Later I raised the fee to $1,500 for features and $3,000 for centerfolds. This was much less than *Playboy*. But why pay more? We always had more models than we could use. Some people— never our regular readers—argued that our models were not as good-looking as those in *Playboy* or *Penthouse*. That argument had no validity, because many of our models appeared in those magazines after posing for *Hustler* first.

By the time the fifth issue came around, I had developed my own philosophy of what our models should look like. I wanted them to be the "girl next door." *Playboy*'s Hugh Hefner had always said that he wanted that same look, but every woman who appeared in his magazine was the archetype for the unattainable, perfect goddess: 5'8", 36-24-36, usually blond. "Is that what *your* neighbor looks like?" I thought to myself. It seemed to me that the working stiffs I knew had fantasies about women who were a little more attainable. I chose models who did not have extensive professional portfolios, young women who really *were* the girl next door. These women ranged from tall to short; were blond and brunette, large-breasted and small-breasted. In other words, they were *real* women, the kind a guy might actually meet or work with.

As I struggled to establish the right look for the women whose photos appeared in *Hustler*, I also began to think about what people wanted to read about. My guiding principle was "give them what they want." I wanted to respond to people as they really were, not what others thought they were or should be. The question I had to face right away was whether the magazine ought to include lifestyle issues, movie reviews, and interviews with mainstream figures, as *Playboy* did. My instinct was to try something different. It seemed to me that if the theme and focus of a magazine is sex, then its whole content ought to serve that purpose. If a guy is going to jerk off looking at a centerfold, does he care about what kind of stereo to buy? I wanted a sex magazine free of pretense and full of fantasy, fiction, satire, and biting humor. I wanted to offend everyone on an equal-opportunity basis. I decided to run cartoons lampooning blacks, whites, Jews, Christians, rich, and poor. It didn't matter to me whom I offended. I wanted to provide a forum for the kind of dark humor that characterized the mills, factories, and workplaces of ordinary people. Humor had always been an escape valve for them, a way to let off steam when life was hard.

The November 1974 issue was a watershed, the first in which *Hustler* featured a so-called "pink shot." The quality of the printing and photography was finally coming together, and the directness and naturalness of the nudes had improved immeasurably. My idea of featuring female genitalia was fully realized. In the November issue the model's genitals were explicitly photographed—her vagina open like a flowering rose, fragile and pink. As the November issue went out, I hoped against hope that it would sell. Everything was riding on it. If I was right about the photos and editorial content, this issue would be a blockbuster. If people didn't like the new explicitness, I was doomed. Because of the long delay between the printing of an issue and its distribution, sale, and the collection of revenues, I had nearly run out of money. Sales of *Hustler*'s first four issues had been low and did not recoup costs. By the time December arrived, I still didn't know that November had been a success. I was already working on the February 1975 issue. I decided that if I was going to go down, I'd go down smoking. With the precedent already set, I turned the heat up in that issue with the magazine's most explicit centerfold so far, combined with a photo spread featuring an adolescent-middle-age fantasy: a very young woman with an older man.

All the while I squeezed every last dollar out of the Hustler Clubs. There would be no February issue if I couldn't somehow raise the cash from the clubs. I knew by now that I had to make the magazine go or I would end up in jail. The taxman was breathing down my neck. Although the Hustler Clubs were my only source of cash, I was spending almost all of my time on the magazine. I was caught in a vicious circle: I had to manage the clubs to raise the money to publish the magazine, but while managing the magazine I didn't have time to manage the clubs. I couldn't do it any longer. Finally I called in an old friend, Bill Abrams, and asked him to take over management of the clubs.

He owed me one. Abrams, an ex-con, was the only man I trusted to do the job. He wouldn't bullshit me, and neither would he steal anything. With Bill on the job I could concentrate on the magazine and creditors. Most of the people I owed money to knew I wouldn't cheat them. I put them on what I called my "later on plan." If that didn't work, I put them on my "TLC plan" and gave them a lot of attention but very little money. I made a mental note of those people who carried me and did my best to return the favor in later years. In the meantime, the latest issue went to press.

The February 1975 issue caused a furor. When it was shipped from the printer, some 40 percent of my wholesalers, including all of Canada, refused to carry it. While I was still reeling from the news, I learned that my local wholesaler in Columbus, Roger Scherer, was not going to put out the issue, either. Worse, Scherer, then president of the Council of Periodical Distributors Association, was getting ready to send a memo to all its members advising them not to handle the February issue. At all costs, I needed to stop that memo. I got Scherer's secretary on the phone and told her that I needed to see him immediately, that it was a matter of life and death. I had never met him and had no personal relationship to which I could appeal. He wasn't eager to see me, but reluctantly agreed. I showed up at his office determined to do or say whatever it took to gain his support. I sat down in front of his desk and got right to the point: "Don't bust my balls!" Scherer wasn't used to people as direct as me and suppressed a smile. "I just found out that 50,000 copies were bounced from Canada. If you don't put it out, and your members don't put it out, I'll go broke," I pleaded. I was willing to cry if it would help. "And you don't want me to go broke," I added optimistically. He shifted around in his chair and looked uncomfortable. A tense conversation ensued.

Scherer told me that he didn't want to put the issue out because he was afraid his people would get arrested. He was also uncomfortable, he said, with its explicitness and thought it was bad for both personal and business reasons. He said, "My image is at stake, and my company might suffer." I didn't care about his image, and I knew that if he released it, the issue would sell big, and we would both make a lot of money. Finally he said that he would release it if the officer in charge of the Columbus vice squad would promise not to arrest any of his dealers. He probably assumed that it would be the end of the matter—that I would give up and go away. He was wrong. I stood up and said, "Okay, I'll have him call you."

I walked out of Roger Scherer's office like a man on a mission. I got in my car, drove to an adult bookstore and bought three hard-core pornographic magazines, put them in my briefcase, and headed for the police station. There I asked for the vice-squad commander, got directions to his office, walked in, and introduced myself. I told him that I owned the Hustler Club downtown. "I know who you are," he said. Then I told him that I had started a magazine. He said he knew that, too. His tone didn't reveal what he thought of me. I took a deep breath and said, "I'm new to the publishing business, and I want to stay within the obscenity guidelines. I'd like you to look at the February issue of *Hustler* and tell me what you think." I handed him a copy that I had in my briefcase. He leafed through it and paused. I then said, "Do you want to see some real hard stuff?" I pulled the other magazines from my briefcase. He glanced at the covers, pulled his desk drawer open, and took out several magazines similar to the ones I had in my hand. He explained that they were there because he was trying to decide whether to arrest the dealers who sold them. "*Hustler* is tame compared with what's on the market," he said, and added, "I don't see a problem." I wanted to hug him, but decided it wasn't a good idea. "Would you mind repeating that to my distributor?" I asked. He agreed. I immediately got Roger Scherer on the phone and had the commander talk to him directly. The issue went out, and the damning memo was never sent.

The February 1975 *Hustler* nearly sold out, in spite of the fact that Canadian distributors still refused to carry it. By April I was grossing over $500,000 an issue. All of a sudden sales, circulation, and profits were beginning to skyrocket. And none too soon. Right before the taxman was due to come knocking on my door, I paid off all my back payroll, withholding, and sales taxes. The IRS and the State of Ohio had successfully financed the start of *Hustler* magazine. I would have sent them a thank-you note, but I didn't think they'd have considered it funny. By June the clubs were no longer financing the magazine, but were being financed by it. In fact, the Hustler Clubs had become a hindrance. It was time to make another leap and get out of the bar business. I began to look for a buyer. A new chapter of my life was beginning.

Hustler was on the road to success, but it was a rocky one. My distribution woes were not over after the struggle with Roger Scherer. Capital Distributing was nervous all the time and wanted to review the contents of each issue before shipping it to wholesalers. I found myself flying the pasteups and layouts to meetings with Capital people every month. It was a constant pain in the ass. For my first anniversary issue, instead of celebrating my success, I had to fly to Los Angeles to meet with the huge Drown News Agency. Jack Drown was threatening to drop distribution in San Diego and parts of Orange County. I was afraid that if I lost this huge area, I'd lose the whole state of California. Drown was a close friend of President Richard Nixon, and if Nixon hadn't been forced to resign, Drown might have been the next postmaster general. Drown was very conscious of his public image and thought of me as a threat to his carefully manicured reputation. He was angry at me for an interview I had done in the magazine. Admittedly it was over the top, but it was also intended to be tongue-in-cheek. He had no sense of humor, hadn't read the whole interview, and thought I was some kind of pervert. When we sat down to talk, the first thing he said to me—with utter disgust—was, "What kind of person would say the kinds of things you do?"

It wasn't the opening line I wanted to hear. I had to convince him to change his mind and proceeded to do everything I could to placate him. I took the humble approach. I told him that I was new in the business, that I had made a serious mistake, and that I would never do it again. I acted like a chastened child. I told him that if he did not distribute *Hustler*, it would go out of business and I'd go down. He was a much tougher sell than Roger Scherer. But Drown was the kind of paternalistic guy who liked contrite people. He finally softened up and eventually relented. I think he was making too much money on *Hustler* to throw it away for a reason as trivial as principle. In the end he was a practical man.

I worked my ass off to get other wholesalers and distributors to accept *Hustler*. Ordinarily they paid little attention to the titles they carried, but some went over *Hustler* with a magnifying glass, looking for some reason to censor or ban it. But there were always those who were more interested in making money than in trying to further their own conceptions of public morality. The majority of wholesalers never paid much attention to what they carried. They just put *Hustler* out and watched it sell. And it sold very well. Issues were beginning to sell out completely. The wholesale magazine distribution network, despite its size, is clannish and prone to gossip. Word spread quickly that there was a hot new publication available. Many wanted to get on the bandwagon and share in the success. There is nothing that will change a person's moral outlook faster or more completely than money in large amounts.

Hustler's success was assured with the August 1975 issue. I was already making a handsome profit, but that issue made me a millionaire. In the spring of 1975 I was approached by an Italian paparazzo with some sensational photos. They were astonishing nudes of the former first lady, Jacqueline Kennedy Onassis. The photographer had spent several days in a small boat off the Greek island of Skorpios watching the private estate of Jackie and her shipping-magnate husband. The photographer was amply rewarded for his patience. With a huge telephoto lens, he captured a series of photos in which Jackie could be clearly seen in all her naked glory. She had walked out of her house with nothing more than a towel in her hand and a good suntan. The paparazzo took forty-eight full-color shots, with full front and rear nudity, leaving nothing to the imagination. The pictures had already run in the Italian magazine *Playmen*, and fuzzy reproductions had showed up in couple of small sex-oriented rags in New York. But for all practical purposes, no one in the United States had seen or heard of them. The photos were first offered to *Playboy* and *Penthouse*. Both declined. The Kennedy name was powerful, and the two publications were probably afraid that the political climate was poor (Ted Kennedy was a presidential contender) or that mainstream advertisers would object. Their loss was my gain. Surely they must have known that any magazine that published the photos would be a huge commercial success.

I quickly negotiated a price. I had an advantage, because *Playboy* and *Penthouse* had already turned him down. I bought them for $18,000—the best investment I ever made. My attorneys thought I was not at risk in printing them because Jacqueline Onassis was a public figure (now literally) and would not want to litigate such a high-profile matter. I selected five of the best photos and ran four of them full-page, along with a brief biographical article. The pictures had been taken in 1971, when she was forty-one years old, but she was still elegant-looking and slim. I had high expectations for sales and printed an extra 250,000 copies.

The Jackie O issue leaped off the newsstands. I sold a million copies in a matter of days. Every major newspaper and newsmagazine in the country ran articles on *Hustler*. *Time* and *Newsweek* trumpeted the news of the sensational photos. The *Charlotte Observer* carried an article saying, "Don't be shocked if you see a gray-haired grandmotherly type buying a copy of the August issue of *Hustler*, the national men's magazine. That's the issue that has five color photos of Jacqueline Kennedy Onassis in the nude, and local bookstores say the magazine has become strikingly popular—ignoring sex and age boundaries—since the latest issue hit the stands Monday." Indeed, it *was* crossing boundaries. Retailers were reporting that 60 percent of the sales were to women. As one reported, "We've even had little old ladies buying the magazine. They want to see Jackie, too." In Columbus, a local TV station, WBNS, interviewed a woman who ran a sidewalk newsstand. "How're those *Hustler* magazines selling?" the reporter asked. "Like hotcakes!" the woman replied. "Anybody important buying 'em, like, ha-ha, Governor Rhodes?"

the reporter asked, never expecting an affirmative answer. "Well, as a matter of fact . . ." A few minutes earlier, another television reporter, with cameraman in tow, had caught the governor in the act of buying a copy at a hotel gift stand.

The governor of Ohio, James Rhodes, *had* bought a copy. Slightly chagrined, he explained that he had really bought it for himself, but only in the interest of "scholarship." Rhodes had written a book on Mary Todd Lincoln and was working on one about Rachel Jackson. First ladies were his specialty. He thought he might get around to doing one on Jackie Onassis, he said. I'm sure those photos contributed greatly to his research. I'm still looking for that book.

The amazing success of the Jackie O issue created a new and unexpected problem for *Hustler*—getting the sexually explicit magazine printed every month. As I soon came to realize, there were only a few presses in the country that could handle the volume. Always looking for the best price and terms, I signed a lucrative temporary agreement in September 1975 with the Dayton Press. I didn't realize it, but I was about to set off a "morality versus need-to-eat" controversy. When I negotiated with Dayton Press for *Hustler*, it was only printing mainstream titles. Among them were *Newsweek, Ladies' Home Journal, Redbook,* and *Reader's Digest.* When word leaked out that Dayton had agreed to print *Hustler*, all hell broke loose. Within days the Greater Dayton Association of Southern Baptists (a pastors' group) sent Dayton Press executives an outraged letter, condemning them for their decision to print my magazine. How could they stoop so low, it said, as to force their church members—many of whom worked at the Dayton facility—to choose between their moral convictions and the need to make a living?

In the end, dollars defeated conservative Baptist convictions. Southern Baptist Paul Sanders, who had worked for Dayton Press for thirty years, said, "It boils down to economics. It bothers me that some people could complain like this when there's people on the street that aren't working. This is bringing in the work. I know it's not for a child to see, but what's better, a full stomach or an empty one?" The *Dayton Daily News* weighed in with its own indirect endorsement of *Hustler* by saying, "After all the moral indignation it is, after all, a matter of dollars and cents." The reporter noted that the old "G-rated" magazines Dayton was publishing were experiencing huge drops in circulation. In one year the *Ladies' Home Journal* press run had plummeted by more than one million. I watched the whole situation with amusement, especially when I learned that good Baptists were sneaking press copies of the centerfolds out of the plant, and others were plainly enjoying the controversy.

Two months after negotiating my deal with Dayton Press, and still enjoying the publicity of the Jackie O issue, *Hustler* was international news. I was besieged with requests for interviews from publications all over the globe. Even the conservative *Wall Street Journal* took notice of my success and dispatched reporter Frederick

Klein to Columbus to do a story. In a December 1975 article Klein tried to account for the fact that *Hustler* was already more widely read than such long-established titles as *Esquire*. He offered this formula:

> Start off with eight grades of formal school-
> ing and no background in the field. Appoint
> your girlfriend and brother, both similar-
> ly inexperienced, to key posts. Set up in
> Columbus, which offers none of the profes-
> sional services that magazines are supposed
> to need. Aim at a blue-collar audience but
> charge $1.75 an issue and $2.25 in December
> and January; substantially more than the
> competition. Turn off potential advertisers,
> and others, with girlie photos that beg the
> description "sexually explicit," and cartoons
> and stories of the type that used to circulate
> only surreptitiously. What you would have is
> *Hustler*, which is not only the fastest-grow-
> ing men's magazine around but one of the
> fastest-growing magazines of any kind, ever.

Klein was right: I did charge more, I did turn off advertisers, and I was more sexually explicit. What he didn't understand is that all these factors were part of a deliberate strategy. Even *Playboy* and *Penthouse* had trouble with many advertisers, in spite of the fact that their content was mild compared with that of *Hustler*. I knew that I had to be more explicit to appeal to the market I wanted to serve. What I believed, and what turned out to be true, was that people would pay a little more to get what they wanted. If the price of explicitness was a lack of advertisers, so be it. I knew I could recoup the revenue by charging a higher price. In doing so, I could make my readers happy and insulate myself from the censorship of the advertising marketplace. Without advertisers I didn't have to compromise. Rather than cater to a small market of big advertisers, I decided to appeal to what I considered to be my real market: the large body of readers who bought *Hustler* every month. I am a real egalitarian—readers get to decide what they want by voting for it with their dollars. And they voted in large numbers.

On December 31, 1975, I went to bed knowing I had done the impossible. I had broken every rule in the book and succeeded. I had made *Hustler* a success in a market nobody knew existed. I had aimed at the "Archie Bunkers" of America—the men who liked their beer, bourbon, sex, and humor straight—and hit the bull's-eye. My hillbilly instincts had carried me through. My critics thought I had no sophistication whatsoever. What they failed to see was that I had no bullshit in me, either. Sure, I had the gift of con—always had—but I never deluded myself when it came to my audience. The proof was on the nightstand next to me—a check from Capital Distributing for $1,200,000.

5.
An Infallible Instinct

In LIGHT OF THE FACT THAT MANY PUBLIC FIGURES *have chosen to crucify me, I have often been tempted to ask them the age-old question: Who do you say that I am? Over the years, people have answered that question in two distinct ways. There hasn't been much middle ground. One segment of society seems to think of me as a seedy, dirty old man in some back room grinding out pornography. Another group—a much smaller one—sees me as a civil libertarian, someone who has stood up for freedom and the Constitution; someone who has paid a price but brought the process along. The office I'm sitting in today is part of a suite of rooms reserved for my personal use. One of the rooms is a media center. The television in that room is hooked up to a cable service. Today on that cable you can see sex that is more explicit than what you could see in the pages of* Hustler *twenty years ago. I have been at the very center of the constitutional fight to defend every American's right to view whatever he or she desires. I didn't choose that fight, but I fought it nevertheless, and in the process I have helped to protect the rights of every citizen—even those who revile me. I didn't intend to become a crusader for the First Amendment; I hadn't even read the Constitution. But a judge in Cincinnati made me want to read it, and when I did, I discovered that the Founding Fathers did not equivocate when it came to matters of free speech and free choice.*

Since Hustler's inception I have spent much of my time in and out of the nation's courtrooms on various obscenity and libel charges. In one sense I was very much alone in this process. The mainstream press was always willing to enjoy the hard-won freedoms I helped win for them in court, but they seldom had the courage to stand by me in my time of trouble. But in another sense I was not alone. I had a companion, a partner in crime, a soul mate. She made the process bearable, even if she could not make it enjoyable. As I think back, I wonder, "How would it have been possible without her?" It is a question I cannot answer—and would not want to. When you love someone, and are loved in return, even the worst times and circumstances cannot destroy you.

x x x

While it is true that I had innumerable sexual unions, several girlfriends, and an ill-fated marriage after my breakup with Peggy, none of them involved deep feelings, enduring love, or the possibility of a long-term commitment. I was capable of affection and gave it, but I kept a portion of my heart in reserve. I was unwilling to be monogamous and unable to stay with any one woman for long. My clubs, and later *Hustler* magazine, were my real mistresses. I didn't have much energy left over for relationships. I found sex energizing and life-renewing, but I didn't need to get married to have it. It never occurred to me that I needed a special person in my life, and I certainly did not seek one. But it happened anyway.

I met her at my own Hustler Club in Columbus, Ohio. It was the summer of 1971. I had been circulating around the state, visiting the clubs, when I dropped in one evening and sat down at the bar with my brother, Jimmy. A cute little brunette with a gorgeous body was dancing. She had an unusual presence, full of energy and sensuality, but she didn't look to be over fifteen years old. I asked Jimmy, "Where did she come from?" He replied, "I just hired her." I said, "How old is she?" He said, "Eighteen." I said, "Bullshit!" After the girl was through dancing, I had her sent up to my office. She came in, stood just inside the door, and said, "Do you want to see me, sir?" I said, "How old are you?" She replied, "I'm nineteen." I gave her the same reply I'd given to Jimmy: "Bullshit!" She was a little rattled, but pulled an ID from her purse and handed it to me. Even an amateur could see it had been tampered with. The name on the license was "Althea Leasure." "Why don't you just tell me the truth?" I said. She paused. "I need this job—and anyway, I'm *almost* eighteen." "How old are you?" I repeated. "Seventeen and a half," she replied, glancing at the floor. I looked her up and down. She seemed street-smart and vulnerable at the same time.

Althea was actually born on November 6, 1953, in Marietta, Ohio. As I got to know her, I began to unravel the events of her tortured life. I was amazed that this poised, independent seventeen-year-old had survived at all, much less long enough to come and work for me. Her story read like a dime-store novel, full of tragedy, violence, lurid details, and unlikely circumstances. When Althea was nine years old, her father shot and killed her mother, her mother's best friend, her grandparents, and then himself. In an instant she and her siblings were orphaned, and then in a matter of days were split up and parceled out to reluctant relatives. Althea— alone, confused, and still numb from the horror of her parents' violent deaths—spent a brief time with an aunt in Columbus and was then sent to a local children's home. She described the place to me as a "hellhole," where she was sexually molested and subjected to the discipline of a stern, prisonlike regime. "The nuns used to push my face into their crotch," she said. "I rebelled. That place turned me into a horrible person." After one too many fights and a protracted campaign of resistance against the sexual terrorism of the place, she was sent away to an aunt's house in Fort Lauderdale, Florida.

After two months in Florida, Althea wore out her welcome and was shipped back to her aunt in Columbus. Again, this turned out to be a brief, troubled visit. Althea ended up in another fight, and this time punched her aunt in the face. The altercation only served to perpetuate her ping-pong existence, and she was bounced to yet another relative, an older sister who turned out to be just another way station. The sister, apparently without regret, passed her on to a second orphanage, this time in Xenia, Ohio. By now prepubescent but worldly-wise, Althea was using makeup, shaving her legs, wearing panty hose, and dressing provocatively. The second orphanage, puritanical as the first, took away her makeup, imposed a dress code, and told her to stop shaving her legs. Under this new and even stricter regime she became a habitual runaway.

True to its carceral mentality, the second orphanage had its equivalent of a penitentiary's "hole." They called it "isolation" and put Althea in it regularly. She returned the favor by running away every time they let her out. A sad dance was repeated time and again: flight, pursuit, capture, isolation. It was a grinding existence in which Althea learned independence, gained street smarts, nurtured defiance, and developed a dual nature of tough-guy bravado and little-girl vulnerability. Finally, when she was fifteen, and after innumerable stints in "isolation," she ran away for good. By this time Althea had figured out where she could flee and fit in without being noticed, so she hitchhiked to the neighborhood surrounding Ohio State University in Columbus. The area was full of runaways who were indistinguishable from the thousands of students who attended OSU. Within a few days she had found a boyfriend and moved into his apartment. She celebrated her sixteenth birthday with him, smoking grass and tripping on acid. Happy but indiscreet, she was busted, convicted, and sent to a youth-authority detention center for two months. After two orphanages, however, "kidprison" seemed an easy place.

Althea was released from detention on Christmas Eve and went to live with another sister. The youth authority had refused to let her go back to her boyfriend, a decision that irked her not so much because she liked him but because she didn't want to be told what to do. Two weeks later, on the first day she could get into court, she petitioned the judge to declare her an emancipated minor. He agreed. The next day she moved out of her sister's apartment, dropped out of school, quit a part-time job, and moved back into the university district. She had a small trust fund from her father's life insurance, and now that she was an "adult" she could begin collecting it. It was enough to pay her rent and provide $50 a week for food and expenses. With independence and time on her hands, those expenses included drugs. The OSU campus area was saturated with drug-heads, dope dealers, and shooting galleries. It was too much temptation for a bored, unhappy girl. Althea was soon smoking grass daily, experimenting with psychedelics, and—more ominously—shooting up heroin. Within a few weeks she was busted again, this time with all the paraphernalia of a heroin addict (but no heroin) in her apartment. She was put on probation, and on the advice of her lawyer moved out of the university area. Her sister worked at the Hustler Club in Columbus and suggested that Althea audition.

By the time Althea went to work at the Hustler Club, she was ready to channel a portion of her considerable energy into something constructive. She was well suited for the role of go-go dancer and impressed Jimmy with her combination of makeup, false eyelashes, high-heeled boots, and—most of all—her aura of sexuality. She didn't mind if men looked at her as a sex object, and felt she had somehow failed if they didn't. In spite of her youthful appearance, which concerned me, I could see that there was something special about her. She was close to eighteen, so I decided to keep her employed, a decision I wouldn't have made ordinarily. Something inside me wanted her around. As she stood in my office that day—I can still picture it—I knew I had to get to know this woman. If she had been anyone else, I would have fired her on the spot. But I just couldn't bring myself to do it. A few moments of silence passed, and then I said to her, "You can stay." She said, "Thank you, sir," and turned to go out. As she passed through the door, I called out, "You wanna go out after closing?" "Maybe," she replied, and disappeared down the stairs.

She was coy about it, or at least pretended to be, but she did agree to go out with me that night. Usually when I took somebody out after hours, it was for sex and partying—and Althea and I did end up in bed—but something different happened that night. We talked. I found out that this near-eighteen-year-old was an incredibly strong person, emotionally and intellectually able to hold her ground. She didn't mince words and was astoundingly honest. I liked this girl. More than that, I respected her.

Over the following months I took careful note of Althea's loyalty, energy, and ambition. She had obviously made up her mind to learn all she could about my business and make herself indispensable. I wasn't sure what she thought of me at first. I paid a lot of attention to her, but for a while she probably thought I considered her a good fuck, and little else. It wasn't true. She fascinated me. The weeks went by uneventfully, with the exception of one weekend when I got a call informing me that she had been taken to the hospital to have her stomach pumped. She had overdosed on some pills her girlfriend had given her. She was all right, but I made a point to go visit her in the hospital. That simple gesture made her feel loved and cared for. No one had really done much for her in the past. I told her that I was going to promote her to "den mother" of the Columbus club and put her in charge of managing the other dancers. She gave me a broad smile, a warm kiss, and promised me she would do a good job.

Althea did more than a good job; she was outstanding. I promptly promoted her to "senior den mother" in charge of all three hundred dancer-hostesses in the state. I got her a car, and she began traveling between the clubs as an itinerant manager: teaching new dancers how to dress, wear their hair and makeup, walk, talk, and dance. All the while, she was observing every detail of my operations, scrutinizing the managers, checking the registers, keeping an eye on inventories, and noticing how records were kept. It didn't take her long to become an expert. Finally she came to me one night and said, "Larry, I'm ready to manage a club." "What!" I said, not doubting that she could do it, but surprised by her boldness. "I'll be the best manager you ever had because from what I've seen, you don't have anyone as good as I am!" I looked at her for a moment and then began to grin. I thought to myself, "I'll put her in charge of my worst club and see what she can do." And I did.

At the time I still owned Whatever's Right in Dayton, and it was the weakest club in my chain. In fact, it was losing money. I took Althea down to the club and introduced her to the outgoing manager. Then I taught her how to clear the registers, order liquor, take inventory, handle payroll, and make bank deposits. I handed her the keys and said, "Good luck, girl." She didn't need it. The very first week she was in charge, revenues went up. She threw herself into the task, holding staff meetings, hiring new dancers, firing the bad ones, cleaning up the place, and coddling customers. In a matter of weeks she had completely turned the place around. In a couple of months it was making a profit. She did such an outstanding job that it soon became apparent to me that her talents could be put to good use in other clubs. I created a new position for her: roving troubleshooter. She would circulate to my most problematic locations, assess the situation, make changes, and move on. Althea became my eyes and ears.

As Althea's responsibilities grew, so did our relationship. It seemed that I had not only found a woman of unusual capabilities, but one who was entirely loyal and had no interest in judging or changing me. I was comfortable around her. I could be myself without penalty or excuse. We could go out together to a nice French restaurant or grab a greasy old hamburger. It didn't matter. She had no expectations, no agenda to impose. I soon found myself spending a lot of time with her: fishing, horseback riding, an occasional trip. It was these nonsexual things that brought us close and made the friendship so satisfying. We had good sex, too—sometimes great sex—but I had been with hundreds of women who were better in bed than Althea, and I hadn't been in love with any of them. But I was falling in love with her. Althea's name, I have been told, either comes from the Greek verb "to heal" or the nouns "truthfulness" or "dependableness." She was all this to me and more.

The relationship that developed between Althea and me was not an ordinary one in any sense. It did not conform to conventional models of morality; in fact, it flew in the face of American middle-class orthodoxy. From the beginning Althea understood that I would not be sexually exclusive. I would always have other women, and she knew it. What she also knew was that I would not form other friendships as deep as our own. No one else could be as close to me as she was. She understood the difference between fucking and love, knew that I loved her, and didn't care who I fucked. Her only rule was this: I could have all the sex I wanted, but I couldn't kiss any other woman but her. If she caught me kissing another woman—and on a few occasions she did—she would kick me in the ass and remind me of the rule. I, in turn, knew that she was bisexual and didn't care if she had relationships with women. Althea, who didn't seem to desire other men, definitely desired other women. I didn't mind. I don't know if I would have been jealous if she had slept with other men. I suppose, in the name of consistency, I would have had to have been as open-minded as she was. But I never had to face that test. We recognized each other's proclivities. I slept with a lot of women; she slept with a lot of women. It worked. We were happy. I asked her to move in with me.

The day-to-day intimacy of sharing a house destroys some relationships, but living with Althea only deepened my attachment to her. She was the only person I had ever considered a true soul mate. How could I not love someone who was so deeply committed to me? Althea wanted so desperately to have someone to hold on to and believe in. Even when I was wrong, it was all right with her. She clung to me as though her life depended on it. I had the feeling sometimes that if she stopped believing in me, it would threaten her whole existence. She once said that if things ever got really bad, she would be willing to go out on the street and sell her body to help me raise cash. It was her way of expressing absolute fidelity, but the words she chose to express it made me sad. She carried a lot of emotional baggage from her traumatic childhood. On the one hand she was a cool, competent manager; on the other she was a little girl who slept with stuffed toys and liked to please adults. I remember one occasion when her childlike quality was particularly evident. Althea kept a pet bird named Wilbur. One day when we came home, we found Wilbur dead, lying at the bottom of his cage. Like a child of ten, Althea placed the bird in a box, held a funeral service, and buried it in the backyard.

In her fourth year of employment, at the ripe old age of twenty-one, Althea had accomplished just about everything she could for the Hustler Clubs. In the meantime I was struggling to get *Hustler* magazine out every month with a full-time staff of three and a half dozen part-timers. I needed help in the worst way. I had been thinking for some time that Althea's energy could be put to better use working on the magazine. I was considering selling the clubs but hadn't told her yet. Eventually I made up my mind to appoint her to the magazine staff, and one Friday night over dinner I broached the subject. I said, "If I told you I wanted you to quit the clubs, that this was your last night, and I wanted you to come in and run the magazine, what would you say?" She looked at me with a combination of shock and disbelief, as though I had just pissed on her shoe. "What!" Fumbling for words, she blurted out, "I can't do it! I don't know anything about running a magazine! I can run your clubs but not your magazine!" I ignored her protests. I knew she could do it. I said to her, "Monday you start running the magazine."

Two days later she was at the magazine's office. Her title was "managing director," and of course she didn't know one thing about what she was supposed to be managing. She spent the whole day talking to the other employees, finding out what their jobs were. She didn't know an art director from an associate editor. In

a few days it was clear that the scope of her responsibilities exceeded even my confidence in her, and we
talked about what should be done. I decided to name a
new managing director and promoted her to executive
editor. This quick promotion made the phrase "mete-
oric rise" seem inadequate. But she was up to the task.
What she lacked in experience and formal training, she
made up for with hard work and an infallible instinct.
As executive editor, Althea acted as a liaison between
me and the editorial staff, was responsible for approv-
ing payment for the freelancers from whom we bought
articles, and screened some of the editorial material
before it got to me. After a while I trusted her to look at
virtually everything with an eye toward what was worth
my attention and what wasn't. She was my gatekeeper.

Althea had an intuitive understanding of what I
liked and didn't like. She would read material before it
got to me, and if she was sure I wouldn't like it, reject
it outright. If she thought I might like it with certain
changes, she would send it back and ask that they be
made. If she didn't like it herself but thought I would,
she would send it to me with a note explaining what
she would change. The remarkable thing about this
process is that she seldom erred in her judgment of
what pleased me. She understood me thoroughly and
shared my dislike of bullshit. Althea and I had an in-
depth appreciation of what our readers liked and
always tried to avoid even the slightest hint of pretense, technical jargon, or what she called "fourteen-
letter words." She came to describe her job as "killing
bullshit before it gets to Larry." She was good at it. She

had an uncanny sense of what appealed to our readers, and in an era in which no other men's magazine employed a woman as a top-level executive, she added a dimension that they lacked.

In spite of her initial apprehension, Althea never looked back. She helped transform *Hustler*, and in the process transformed herself. The change from night-club dancer and hostess to executive editor of a multi-million-dollar publishing corporation was more than a change of jobs. It affected her in deep ways. When she was in the clubs, she went all out in her attempt to be every man's dream, an object of desire. She wore low-cut satin dresses with push-up bras, ratted-out hair, false eyelashes, heavy makeup, and spike heels. It was a look she later described as "vulgar." As a dancer she got angry if men didn't objectify her. As an executive she got angry if they did. Her whole appearance changed. She started wearing little or no makeup and dressing in classy, expensive clothes. She began to think of herself as a person with an intellect.

As her intellectual confidence grew, she became disdainful of the prevailing wisdom that asserted women were not qualified to edit a men's magazine. She considered the premise a myth. In her view, all women were potentially better men's magazine editors than men were. She pointed out that in a sexist society, women spend most of their lives trying to understand men, keep ahead of them, and figure out what turns them on. "The average man," she said, "likes to read about someone else having a good time in bed so he can get turned on by it. Women like reading about *how* to give a man a good time." She thought that women knew more about sex than men. She used to say that a woman can get laid a hundred times in one day if she wants it, but a man may spend all day and night trying to get one girl in bed. Sexually experienced women, she thought, were the ultimate authorities on men. In her experience the average man who projected a masculine and confident image in public was often insecure in bed. She understood those insecurities and saw to it that the pages of *Hustler* addressed them in creative and satisfying ways.

As my relationship with Althea grew, so did my wealth. In January 1976 I decided that we ought to move into a home and neighborhood more befitting my financial success. After a brief search we found a place that suited us perfectly. It was in an upper-crust section of Columbus, Ohio, called Bexley. When it was announced that I would buy it, a small furor ensued. The mansion had once been owned by the governor of the state. *Columbus Monthly*, a local magazine, carried an article with the title, "The Hustler Goes to Bexley," complete with cartoon caricatures of Althea and me on the cover, posed in front of the mansion. Althea was portrayed in a provocative nightie, sprawled on the grass with her arm around my leg. I was depicted with a copy of *Hustler* magazine in my hand, supposedly hawking it to some unseen neighbor. It was an inside joke to anyone who knew the neighborhood. Across the street was the exclusive Columbus School for Girls. One local wag suggested that I would probably be out in front of the school handing out lollipops rather than magazines.

Althea was now known as my "live-in girlfriend," an anomaly in the conservative, predominately Republican neighborhood. According to local sentiment I was "living in sin," but it didn't matter because I had the price of admission. When you have a lot of money, you don't need class. I paid $375,000 for the mansion—a huge sum of money for a house in those days, especially in Ohio. *Columbus Monthly* announced that I would be spending a sum equal to the purchase price on renovating and redecorating the place—I did, and more. When I bought it, the mansion had six bedrooms, a library, a projection room, a wine cellar, two basement recreation rooms, and a huge party room complete with waterfall and koi pond. I renovated everything, added a sauna and steam room, remodeled the bathrooms, and installed a heart-shaped tub for two in the master suite. I replaced all the windows with bulletproof glass. In the basement I built a faux hillbilly cabin, complete with a three-foot replica of the chicken I had violated in my youth. Who said I'm not sentimental?

The Bexley mansion was a symbol of my success, but it also turned out to be a lightning rod. The stone wall and bulletproof glass were prudent additions. The Bexley Brahmins were not overjoyed to have us around. Almost everybody snubbed us, a few were openly hostile, and occasionally some nut would ring my doorbell at three in the morning and make a vague threat. I had an unlisted telephone number, but nevertheless received frequent midnight calls promising God's retribution against me, Althea, and my family. The local police didn't seem much interested in my security problems, so I ended up having to hire my own guards. A loosely organized movement to get *Hustler* out of Ohio, and me out of Bexley, was also begun by one of my "friendly" neighbors, an attorney named Richard Miller. His blond daughter was blunt and typical of the upper-class snobbery—and outright hate—directed toward us. She said simply, "We don't want you people around here." We like to pretend we don't have class prejudice in America, but we do. I know what it feels like, and not many things make me angrier.

With fame and fortune and a high-profile piece of real estate, a whole new set of problems presented themselves. The days of my bar brawls were over, but a new era of legal battles was beginning. It began to dawn on me that it was possible I might be spending as much time in court defending *Hustler* as running it. As *Hustler*'s success grew, it attracted the attention of prosecutors in counties all over Ohio and in several other states as well. For a while I wondered, "Why me?" There was hard-core pornography everywhere, in adult bookstores and magazine stalls, and behind newsstand counters. It eventually dawned on me that the reason I was singled out was the political and social content of the magazine. *Hustler* was political and class-oriented. For example, I had started a feature called "Asshole of the Month," in which I lambasted politicians, religious figures—anyone in the public eye—who I thought were phony or hypocritical. We raked people over the coals in language and cartoon imagery no one had ever had the balls to use in a national magazine before. It really pissed people off. We ran cartoons that were offensive to all racial and ethnic groups. We spared no one. We were entirely bipartisan. We didn't care about your political affiliation. If you were an asshole, we said so. A typical example: We ran one cartoon showing Henry Kissinger, Gerald Ford, and Nelson Rockefeller gang-raping the Statue of Liberty. The vulgar nature of our cartoons and features was a matter of editorial policy. We would intentionally try to offend people. Apparently we succeeded. The Statue of Liberty cartoon made the mayor of Cleveland so angry that he held a press conference to condemn it and then instructed his district attorney to indict us for obscenity.

Of the many legal entanglements to come, the first truly major case was tried in Cincinnati. Althea and I were charged with several criminal violations of Ohio law there, along with my production manager, Al Van Schaik, and my brother, Jimmy. In July 1976 we were indicted for pandering, obscenity, and organized crime—all for publishing *Hustler* magazine. We went through a perfunctory ritual in which we turned ourselves in, were arrested and arraigned, posted bond, and were ordered to appear for trial. Although the charges were ridiculous, the stakes were high. If we were convicted, the maximum penalty was twenty-five years in prison. And the atmosphere in Cincinnati was hostile—to say the least—toward *Hustler*.

Cincinnati was the home of the most aggressive and well-financed antipornography movement in the country and headquarters for an organization called

Citizens for Decency Through Law (CDL). The CDL had been founded and funded by the conservative Catholic and moral crusader (and now convicted felon) Charles H. Keating. Before he fucked the savings and loan industry, Keating tried to prevent the portrayal of fucking in magazines. He employed six full-time lawyers to help root out the "evil" from newsstands and provide legal support to supposedly overburdened prosecutors. Among his services was the reading and viewing of pornographic magazines and films that his organization would analyze, summarize, and make available to prosecutors and legislators. Thus the organization simultaneously provided a vehicle for its staff members to pursue their own obsession with smut in a socially sanctioned way and condemn it at the same time. Freud would have had a field day: several guys sitting around watching porno flicks, saying, "God, that was disgusting—would you rewind the film and play it again?" In addition to reviewing pornographic material, Keating's organization had its own morality squad, a group of dour Catholic mothers who showed up at trials, packing the audience and intimidating juries with silent stares (all the while fingering their rosary beads). To top it all off, Keating's brother, Bill, was president of the city's most influential paper, the *Cincinnati Enquirer*.

Cincinnati was also the fiefdom of its chief prosecutor, Simon Leis, Jr. Leis and I had a long history of animosity. Like Keating, Leis was an ultraconservative Catholic. He was also sexually repressed and a moral crusader. Among the practices he wanted to root out of decent society were those of fellatio and cunnilingus.

As far as I know, he couldn't tell a clitoris from a rutabaga, and it's my guess that Mrs. Leis was an *extremely* tense woman. But I digress. Four years earlier, in May 1972, I had been at Caesar's Palace in Cincinnati with Jimmy and Sam Griffith. Sam had had too much to drink, gotten in an argument with another woman, pulled a gun from her purse, and fired a round into the ceiling. I grabbed the pistol away from her and tried to calm her down. She began to sob, finally collapsing into my lap. The police came, but instead of arresting Sam, they arrested me. I was booked for discharging a firearm in the city. When I was brought to trial, Simon Leis, Jr., was the prosecutor. Both Jimmy and Sam testified that I wasn't the one who'd shot the gun. It didn't matter. Leis based his case on my supposed lack of character and convinced the good citizens of Cincinnati to convict me against the evidence. I served twenty-seven days before being allowed to post bail. Leis, who never let the law get in the way of his zeal, filed a perjury charge against me after I was released. His complaint said that since I had pleaded "not guilty" but was found "guilty" by the jury, I must have perjured myself. This legal absurdity was quickly overturned by a higher court. Still undaunted, Leis filed a *third* charge, accusing me of sodomy! His case: When Sam had collapsed in my lap, she wasn't crying; she was actually performing oral sex on me.

In 1976 drumming up any support for freedom of the press in Cincinnati was difficult. Keating's bluenose influence was everywhere. I was concerned that no one would speak up for the First Amendment in a city dominated by repressed Catholics who intended to retain control of the citizens' morals no matter what the cost—financial *or* ethical. I decided the only way to build resistance to the repression was to organize it myself. I founded an ad hoc organization and called it "Ohioans for a Free Press" (OFP). My idea was to have the OFP sponsor a rally. But promoting it turned out to be a challenge. None of the newspapers in Cincinnati would run a paid advertisement announcing the time and place of the rally. I tried several different strategies to get something published. I submitted an ad that featured a photo of Adolf Hitler, along with a quote from him: "The reorganization of our press has truly been a success . . . divergencies of opinion between members of the government are no longer an occasion for public exhibitions and are not the newspaper's business. We've eliminated that conception of political freedom which holds that everybody has the right to say whatever comes into his head." The ad was turned down by every newspaper in the city. We called the *Cincinnati Post* and asked, "What will you accept?" There was silence on the line. We said, "Will you accept the front page of the Constitution of this country with the addition of a single credit at the bottom that reads, 'Sponsored by Ohioans for a Free Press'?" The paper still refused.

We had the rally anyway. We decided to hold it at the Netherland Hilton in downtown Cincinnati. The lack of advertising had hurt. Instead of having the thousands I had hoped for, only two hundred showed up, including some thirty members of the press. It was something of a mob scene nevertheless. There were several dozen people milling around me with tape recorders, cameras, and notebooks. I finally got them to calm down and ask me one question at a time. They weren't even slightly interested in the issues that my trial raised; their only interest was in discrediting me. They asked me if the OFP was just a front organization for *Hustler*, and whether I was trying to cover up my connection to it. "Of course not!" I shouted at them. "I've never tried to hide my connection or deny that its financial support comes from me. I've supported many causes and organizations, including the Anti-defamation League in this city." They weren't listening. I could feel my anger rising.

One of my employees had a tape recorder. I don't remember much of what I said, but the transcript of that night's rally captured my anger. "We're talking about the censorship of a magazine with three million circulation, sold in twenty-five different countries with an estimated fifteen million readers . . . that's fifteen million voices that have a right to be heard . . . now either we have a free press or we don't. I think that if we *do* have a free press, it's time that the god-damn journalists in this country got some backbone. One of the greatest things that we have as American citizens, goddammit, is the right to be left alone, and me and my readers deserve that right." I had reason to be angry. I felt as though I was under a virtual state of siege. My adopted hometown, Columbus, was relentlessly hostile. An action had been filed against me in Cleveland. It seemed as though all the major cities in

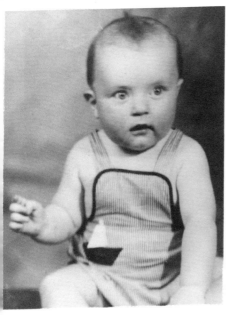

Me as baby in 1942 *(left)*.

Me with my mother, Edith, at the age of two *(bottom left)*.

Posing in my finest at the age of three *(below)*.

Me at the age of eleven with my brother Jimmy, age five (above lef

1955 (above).

In the Navy. Me and buddy in Naples, Italy in 1962 (left).

1972 (below).

The first cover of *Hustler*, July 1974.

One of the infamous Jackie O. photos published in *Hustler*, August 1975.

Jimmy and I at his wedding in Las Vegas *(top left)*.
Jimmy joins me and Althea at our 1976 wedding *(top right)*.
Althea and I in New Orleans in 1977 with daughter Theresa *(bottom)*.

Columbus Ohio mansion, 1977 *(top)*.

Debating Congressman Robert Dornan on Cincinnati television show in 1977 *(middle)*.

Me and Althea at home in Columbus *(below)*.

Althea in 1980 *(left)*.

Althea and I soon after the shooting in 1978 *(below)*.

Phil Donahue, Althea, and m on Mississippi River in 1978 *(bottom)*.

Jerry Falwell talks about his first time.

INTERVIEWER: But your mom? Isn't that a bit odd?

FALWELL: I don't think so. Looks don't mean that much to me in a woman.

INTERVIEWER: Go on.

FALWELL: Well, we were drunk off our God-fearing asses on Campari, ginger ale and soda—that's called a Fire and Brimstone—at the time. And Mom looked better than a Baptist whore with a $100 donation.

FALWELL: My first time was in an outhouse outside Lynchburg, Virginia.

INTERVIEWER: Wasn't it a little cramped?

FALWELL: Not after I kicked the goat out.

INTERVIEWER: I see. You must tell me all about it.

FALWELL: I never really expected to make it with Mom, but then after she showed all the other guys in town such a good time, I figured, "What the hell!"

INTERVIEWER: Campari in the crapper with Mom . . . how interesting. Well, how was it?

FALWELL: The Campari was great, but Mom passed out before I could come.

INTERVIEWER: Did you ever try it again?

FALWELL: Sure . . .

lots of times. But not in the outhouse. Between Mom and the shit, the flies were too much to bear.

INTERVIEWER: We meant the Campari.

FALWELL: Oh, yeah. I always get sloshed before I go out to the pulpit. You don't think I could lay down all that bullshit sober, do you?

Campari, like all liquor, was made to mix you up. It's a light, 48-proof, refreshing spirit, just mild enough to make you drink too much before you know you're schlockboozed. For your first time, mix it with orange juice. Or maybe some white wine. Then you won't remember anything the next morning. Campari. The mixable that smarts.

CAMPARI You'll never forget your first time.

Me with Liz Berriors, my fiancee of five years (left).

The legendary Campari ad featuring Jerry Falwell (top right).

With daughters Theresa (left) and Lisa (right) at Hustler 20th anniversary party in 1994 (above).

My children (left to right): Larry Jr., Lisa and Theresa (left).

Hustler ad parody in 1983: Larry Flynt Goes Broke! (next page).

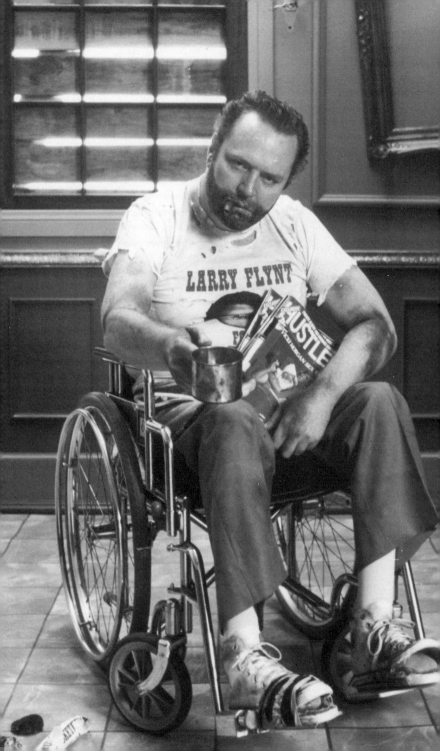

Ohio had reactionary, provincial middle classes, bred to work in the carcinogen-spewing factories located on the outskirts of their towns. They hated *Hustler*. The upper classes were frequently uptight, buttoned-down, and repressed. Keating and Leis were hardly rarities. The middle and upper classes were out to get me. I was under so much pressure in Columbus that I had begun to wonder if *anyone* cared about the fundamental freedoms that Americans supposedly cherished. People didn't seem to get it. My supporters and I began to call Ohio "the state where the dumb come to die."

The pandering and obscenity charges leveled against me were both misdemeanors, carrying a maximum penalty of six months in jail and a $1,000 fine. However, the organized-crime charge was a felony, with a maximum penalty of twenty-five years in prison and a fine of over $10,000. The statute, as originally enacted, was intended to combat the Mafia, but was worded so loosely that "organized crime" could apply to any group of five or more people who "conspired" to participate in any illegal activity. As one of my churlish employees remarked, "If five people in Ohio conspire to cross the street against the light, they can be charged with organized crime, and if found guilty made to serve the maximum sentence of twenty-five years in prison." The conspiracy charges were a bald attempt to raise the stakes and multiply the risk of the lesser charges filed against me. Four people were named in the indictment—but it took five to constitute conspiracy. The fifth "person" was *Hustler* magazine.

The indictments were filed just three years after the 1973 Supreme Court's landmark decision *Miller* v. *California*. In that case the court avoided the difficult task of defining obscenity by relegating the job to those even less qualified than themselves—local courts—and deferring to the concept of "community standards." The frightening implication was that national standards would be systematically brought in line with those of its most conservative citizens. And Cincinnati indeed was, and still is, very conservative. Under the continuing "leadership" of Simon Leis, Jr., the city has prosecuted everyone from the Contemporary Art Center, for its Mapplethorpe exhibition, to Barnes & Noble, for selling *Libido* magazine.

With some apprehension, Althea and I checked into a suite on the twentieth floor of the Stouffer's Hotel. It was to be our home and headquarters during the trial. It had two television sets, one in the bedroom and one in the living room. Althea kicked off her shoes as she walked into the bedroom, turned on the TV, and flopped down on the bed. The evening news was under way. It was Channel 9, the CBS affiliate. "Larry," she called, "there's something about the trial on TV." I ran into the room. On the screen a taciturn local news anchor named Al Schottelkotte was droning on about the upcoming trial. He was saying some unflattering things about me. I wasn't surprised. Schottelkotte's brother James was managing editor of the *Cincinnati Enquirer,* and the *Enquirer*, of course, was run by Charles Keating's brother. It was going to be an uphill fight.

6.
Closet Perverts

WHY IS IT THAT CERTAIN PEOPLE NEED TO CONTROL *others? Why is it that some prosecutors, politicians, and religious leaders want to regulate our loins and our libido? What are they afraid of? There is a widespread belief among many conservatives—one that is seldom openly acknowledged—that if our sexual behavior can be controlled, our whole lives can be brought into submission. According to these people, sex is dangerous. I think sex can be dangerous in a biological sense—AIDS and other sexually transmitted diseases are certainly deadly—but that is not what they are talking about. Sex is dangerous to them in the broader political and social sense. Sex is part of their regime of repression. When pornography threatens or challenges the politics of repressed politicians and religious leaders, it is always condemned, prohibited, and legislated into nonexistence. Silence is the goal of repression. Consequently, the mere fact that I have spoken out has offended those in power. Anyone who dares to make public the language and imagery of sex commits an act of rebellion and says, in effect, "I am outside the reach of your power." Sex is subversive; it smacks of revolt and freedom, and people like Charles Keating and Simon Leis, Jr., feel threatened by it. The repressed always prefer private perversion to public honesty.*

In the Middle Ages a certain frankness about sex was common. By contemporary standards sex was earthy, crude, and unvarnished. Bodies were bodies: sometimes perfumed and beautiful, often flatulent and gross. But above all, they were real. What is it about real bodies, bodies portrayed with openness and honesty, that causes people to hate, prosecute, and imprison others? The sexual aesthetics of common people, especially those from Appalachia, are more like those of the unrepressed masses of the Middle Ages than the sanitized, idealized women of American advertising and Playboy. I've recognized this difference from the beginning, and it has always landed me in trouble. How dare I portray the sexual aesthetics of the "great unwashed"?

As I sit in my office today, my trial for obscenity in Cincinnati seems as though it were a lifetime away. But it is not. The issues are still with us. That trial was emblematic then, and continues to be emblematic, of the great class divide in America.

x x x

My trial in Cincinnati took place in the midst of a highly charged political atmosphere. The judicial climate had taken a decisive turn to the right when, in 1973, the Supreme Court issued a landmark ruling on obscenity: *Miller* v. *California*. Richard Nixon's appointee, Chief Justice Warren Burger, had been leading the court in redefining standards for obscenity in ways I—as did many others—thought were exceedingly dangerous. The Burger Court had recently given local communities the right to establish their own standards for obscenity. Prior to *Miller* v. *California* any community could prosecute a national publication on obscenity charges, but that community had to apply *national* standards in reaching its decision. This meant, for example, that if a jury found a publication guilty of obscenity in one state, the same material would also have to be found obscene by a jury in every other state, since the same standard would have to be applied everywhere.

Miller v. *California* was a case in which Marvin Miller, the owner of a West Coast mail-order business, was convicted of sending unsolicited, sexually oriented ads through the mail. Hearing the case, the Burger court overturned the previous understanding, maintaining that in the future a publication or film need only be found guilty of obscenity in the community in which it was tried. To make matters worse, the court also held that the prosecution need not offer any proof or expert testimony as to what constituted "obscenity." This contravened a long-standing rule of jurisprudence: Juries were not previously presumed to be experts in areas of technical complexity.

At first glance the decision might have seemed like a reasonable one. After all, why shouldn't a community be allowed to determine what type of material it wants to be exposed to? On closer examination, however, it became obvious to me—and to other advocates of the First Amendment—that this decision meant that a publisher of a national newspaper or magazine had to avoid offending the most conservative community in the country or take the chance of being sent to jail for as long as (in some states) sixty-five years. It meant that conservative Kansans could, if they were so inclined, go to court and dictate what liberal New Yorkers could buy in New York. And that is exactly what happened. The city attorney in Wichita, Kansas, prosecuted Al Goldstein—the publisher of *Screw* magazine—on obscenity charges, even though Goldstein lived in New York and published his magazine there.

As I prepared to go to trial, I was faced with a new three-part test for obscenity based on the *Miller* v. *California* decision: 1. Whether the average person applying community standards would find that the work taken as a whole appealed to prurient interest; 2. Whether the work depicted or described, in a patently offensive way, sexual conduct specifically defined (or prohibited) by the applicable state law; 3. Whether the work taken as a whole lacked serious literary, artistic, political, or scientific value. All three tests had to be met to get a conviction, but since "local community standards" applied, it was possible for a jury to be encouraged to ignore the guidelines, believing that they alone could make up their own minds. Given the nature of the community in which I was being tried, I had reason to worry.

My lawyer for the trial was a well-respected, gray-haired, distinguished-looking First Amendment specialist, Harold Fahringer, from Buffalo, New York. His partner, Paul Cambria, represented Jimmy. My staff called Fahringer and Cambria "Batman and Robin." Althea and Al Van Schaik were represented by the portly Charles Kaps, a local attorney chosen for his connections in Cincinnati and his ability to play the part of a "good ol' boy." Fahringer was worried that the jury would distrust out-of-town city slickers.

Fahringer had first achieved prominence as a champion of sexual freedom in 1960, when the American Civil Liberties Union asked him to defend a man who had been arrested on a charge of selling pornographic magazines. Fahringer had taken the case to the New York Supreme Court, which had ultimately declared the law unconstitutional. The case was widely publicized, and other publishers who had similar cases pending lined up to get Fahringer to represent them. The Warren Court was still presiding, and Fahringer enjoyed a good deal of success. I knew Fahringer because I had interviewed him once for *Hustler*.

Fahringer represented pornographers because he considered them to be the ones most likely to have their constitutional rights violated. He passionately believed that people should have the right to enjoy any form of sexual entertainment or activity as long as it did not harm anyone, and as long as it was done privately and with consent. He considered the newsstand the "poor man's library or art museum." The rich and privileged could go to exotic museums and theaters to see erotic art, he held, but the working class had to get its entertainment in magazines and movies. He did not think that any form of literature was capable of producing antisocial behavior.

The prosecution was headed, of course, by Simon Leis, Jr., with assistance from his lackey, Assistant Prosecutor Fred Cartolano. Leis's strong Germanic features and militaristic bearing—he was an ex-Marine—were perfectly appropriate for the role. He was forty-three years old. Cartolano, forty-nine, was swarthy and slim. One wiseass described him as a "wop version of *Star Trek*'s Mr. Spock." Leis had a reputation for bombast; Cartolano was supposed to be the brains. Not that anybody was likely to call Cartolano an intellectual. It's all relative. Both men were Catholic, as was William Morrissey, the pudgy jurist assigned to the trial.

In addition to the obvious players, there were others. In a very real sense the whole conservative community was conspiring against me in ways that were highly effective but often hidden. Cincinnati was a city in which right-wingers seemed to flourish. Six years earlier a group calling itself the Real Friends of the Library had mounted a campaign to remove "objectionable" books from public libraries on the grounds that they were either obscene or written by Communists. The group was supported by a nut named Julius Brown, an outspoken foe of that "grave threat" to national security, fluoridated water. Among the books they wanted banned were Kate Millet's *Sexual Politics* and Edgar Snow's *Red Star Over China*.

Charles Keating was involved in nearly every fascist cause in the city and had worked with Simon Leis since the prosecutor's first election in 1971 to root out all sorts of "evil." If there was an attempt to censor, control, or ban books, magazines, movies, or art exhibits, Keating could usually be found playing a role. Leis admitted that his relationship with Keating had been crucial to most of his obscenity prosecutions. "I suppose I could have gotten along without [him]," he said, "but I would hate to have done so." Keating's organization, Citizens for Decency Through Law, had once named Leis "Prosecutor of the Month" for the state of Ohio for his efforts to ban the Bertolucci film *Last Tango in Paris*. Keating had gushed in his newsletter that "Si Leis is a credit to his family, his church, and his community."

I remember standing in front of my Hustler Club in Cincinnati one night, years before the trial, when a party of well-dressed citizens walked by, ogling an undulating go-go girl dancing in the window. They were all intoxicated and talking loudly. One of the group veered away and started for the front door. He was cursing, saying, "This kind of shit needs to be taken care of." His friends pulled him away and herded him back down the sidewalk. I remembered his face and later found out his name. It was Charles Keating.

In anticipation of the circus to come, Harold Robbins flew into town to lend me his support. I had read his novel *The Carpetbaggers* when I was fifteen. Robbins had been working on a new book, *Dreams Die First*, about the publisher of a successful men's magazine. As part of his research he had called me, and the two of us had become friends. After seeing Simon Leis on television, he formed an opinion: "Simon Leis reminds me of a Marine drill sergeant" (no one had told him yet that he actually had *been* one), "but he reminds me of the kind who, after kicking the shit out of some young recruit, would try to fuck him when making up." My thought exactly.

But Leis would not have the opportunity to kick the shit out of recalcitrant jurors—or, presumably, to fuck them, either—so he had to pick them carefully. He used simple criteria: no jurors under thirty years of age; no intelligent or well-educated jurors; no jurors who read men's magazines or had ever seen a porno movie; and no jurors who believed that an adult should have the right to read anything he or she might want. On the other hand, my defense team wanted younger jurors with a different profile: no one with an ultraconservative religious background; no jurors with clear-cut conservative leanings; and no one whose education and intellectual ability seemed substandard. It seemed that the battle was being fought between two completely different generations with radically different morals.

The problem with selecting jurors for my obscenity trial was primarily the difficulty of finding objective and nonrepressed people. Jurors who were repressed, impotent, frigid, or otherwise sexually frustrated would vote "guilty" for sure. If they didn't, they would have to admit that they had spent all their lives missing out on one of the best things life had to offer. How many people would admit to that? And how many sexually open people could there be in a city that was so frightened by sex? As I looked at the faces of prospective jurors, I wondered about their personal lives and their deepest beliefs. It scared the hell out of me. Were they all like Simon Leis, Jr., and Charles Keating?

After the jury was impaneled, several crucial defense motions had to be heard. The most important was one to admit into evidence several hardcore pornographic magazines plus *Hustler*'s direct competitors: *Playboy*, *Penthouse*, *Oui*, etc. The motion stated that since all these magazines had been sold in Hamilton County during the same time that *Hustler* was indicted—they had a combined circulation of at least 300,000 copies a month—it was reasonable to consider them a gauge by which the level of permissibility in the community could be measured. Fahringer told Judge Morrissey that he intended to prove that the magazines "were sold in virtually every corner of Hamilton County" and that they "contained stories and pictures that were often identical to *Hustler*'s." Morrissey took the heavy box of eighty-six different magazines home with him for the night, promising to deliver his decision the following day.

The next morning in court, Morrissey refused to enter the magazines into evidence, a very unfavorable ruling, siding with the prosecution and upholding the notion that the jury itself was representative of the community and constituted the only gauge necessary for determining community standards. In theory, according to Morrissey, the jury *was* the community.

After rendering his decision, he made an amazing admission in a sidebar conference. In his uniquely strong Ohio accent, he said, "Uh had ah wet dream lass night." Considering his age, that was indeed a remarkable, if somewhat curious, confession. Apparently, he studied those magazines quite carefully.

As the first day of the trial began, on a cold February morning in 1977, I found myself sitting at the defendants' table looking at the stone-faced jury, thinking to myself, "This bunch has a combined IQ of 1." After the jury had sat down and squirmed around in their seats for a minute, Morrissey signaled Leis to begin with the opening statement. Slowly, as befits a man of some bulk, Leis rose and walked up to face the expressionless jurors. He was wearing his Marine combat boots. Without saying a word, his face communicated his feelings. It was contorted into an expression of utter disgust. He began with an apology to the jurors for the task he had to unfold before them. He didn't like it any better than they did, he said, but "it had to be done in order to cleanse the community of worthless, immoral, cheap, pornographic trash that depicts women and men posed together in a lewd and shameful manner; which depicts women and women posed together in a lewd and shameful manner; which depicts men posed with animals in a lewd and shameful manner; and which depicts women posed with animals in a lewd and shameful manner." "I guess that covers the bases," I thought to myself. But animals? Were we reading the same magazine?

As Leis talked, the rage in his voice increased.
Suddenly he paused for dramatic effect. He looked at
the jury with a fierce gaze, and in a tone meant to communicate utter disgust, he added, "And which depicts
Santa Claus in a lewd and shameful manner!" Santa
Claus? You could see the incredulity on the jurors'
faces. Yes. Santa Claus. Leis pulled back a step or two
from the jurors to let the revelation sink in. His face
was flushed with righteous indignation, his neck red.
What kind of man *is* this, he implied, who could commit such sacrilege? I squirmed in my seat. Leis was
referring to a cartoon that depicted Santa with an
impressive erection. The caption suggested that his
huge penis was reason enough to say "Ho, Ho, Ho."
Later Al Van Schaik speculated about the cause of
Leis's indignation: "Of course he believes in Santa
Claus. On Christmas Eve his wife makes him go to bed
early so she can hide the presents."

As Leis sat down, my attorney slowly rose from
his chair, walked toward the jury, and smiled. Harold
Fahringer was the embodiment of genteel charm. With
extreme deference to the jury, he told them how hon-
ored he was to be in their great city and how he knew
they would bring in a just verdict. In between throwing
bouquets he painfully pointed out that in keeping with
the law, the jurors would have to make a distinction
between obscenity and tastelessness; explaining that
for something to be obscene, it must, taken as a whole,
appeal to the average person's prurient interest.
Tastelessness was not a crime, he explained. I sat there,
wondering if the jury was capable of understanding

the word *prurient* and fearful that Leis would provide his own synonyms. Fahringer finished his opening remarks with another compliment to the jury. He was doing some serious ass-kissing.

In contrast to Fahringer's "Mr. Nice Guy" approach, Paul Cambria played the hard-ass, continuing the opening statement for the defense in a tone that was aggressive and almost arrogant. I supposed that Fahringer let him get away with it because he was short, and short guys don't scare people. Cambria carefully explained that during the course of the trial, the defense would prove that *Hustler* was not published in Hamilton County and therefore not subject to obscenity laws there. *Hustler*, he stated, was headquartered in Franklin County, Ohio, printed in Montgomery County, and distributed by Capital Distributing Company, which wasn't even in the state. Yet the indictment, as handed down, charged that the defendants engaged in organized crime (published the magazine) in Hamilton County. The charge was ridiculous, Cambria bellowed. The J. L. Marshall News Company, a magazine wholesaler, handled distribution of *Hustler* in Cincinnati. If anyone was subject to local prosecution, it was Marshall, which had not been charged. In fact, Leis had granted immunity to the hometown distributor in exchange for its testifying on behalf of the prosecution.

Cambria drew out the implications for the jury. If they convicted *Hustler*, any two-bit prosecutor in the country could do the same to any publication anywhere, no matter whether it was *National Lampoon* or

the *New York Times*. I thought to myself, "I hope someone on this jury reads above the comic-book level."
Cambria wound down his statement by saying, "If
these defendants can be convicted on this impover-
ished proof, then none of us is safe."

Judge Morrissey, by ruling against the admissibility of
other adult magazines, had made it impossible to
establish *Hustler*'s place within the wide range of porn
sold in Cincinnati. So in lieu of the magazines, Fahringer attempted to present the jurors with the testimony of a number of expert witnesses. The first expert
he called was Dr. Wardell Pomeroy, a psychologist at
California State University and coauthor of the Kinsey
report. Pomeroy had worked at the Kinsey Institute for
twenty years and assisted in the original survey and its
subsequent updates. He had personally interviewed
more than eight thousand of the eighteen thousand
people included in the groundbreaking nationwide sex
survey. Fahringer pointed out that Pomeroy had conducted hundreds of interviews in Ohio, including
Cincinnati.

Speaking quietly, Pomeroy told the court that he
had read all the *Hustler* issues in question and did
not think the cartoons, photographs, and text would
"appeal to the average person's shameful or morbid
interest in sex." What the jury didn't know, and
probably wouldn't have understood anyway, was that
Pomeroy was advancing a theory held by academics
that went like this: If something depicted in a magazine or film is prurient, the average person is repulsed,

[141]

not turned on by it; on the other hand, if a person is incited to commit a prurient act (like extreme sado-masochism or bestiality) by seeing its depiction, he would, by definition, not be average. It was easy to see, if you understood the theory, that according to this viewpoint, *nothing* was obscene as defined by the Supreme Court.

As Fahringer continued to question Pomeroy, he elicited a statement that was completely the opposite of what he knew Leis wanted to establish in subsequent testimony. "Deviant people, such as rapists and child molesters, seem to comprise that segment of society that is *least* exposed to pornography." Pomeroy did not know how to explain this, only that it was true from his research—which was exhaustive. It wasn't clear to him whether deviants had been denied stimulation of their fantasies in printed form, or whether they just weren't interested in fantasy material. In either case, they were not the primary consumers of pornography. Normal people, Pomeroy asserted, were the main consumers of pornography—overwhelmingly so. To prove the point, Fahringer had him read several excerpts from *Hustler* into the record and comment on them. "These are the concerns of ordinary people," Pomeroy testified.

Leis used his cross-examination of Pomeroy to drive home his disgust for *Hustler*'s content. He wanted to have Pomeroy read a few excerpts he had chosen for him. As Leis paced in front of the witness box, he asked Pomeroy to read (silently) an article dealing with incest. Leis had a few odd mannerisms, and as

Pomeroy reviewed the article, Leis stood for a moment, ducking his head and letting his eyes slide from side to side under his lids. He did this whenever he was particularly outraged. The jury waited while Pomeroy read and Leis emoted. "Have you read the article now?" Leis finally asked. "Yes," Pomeroy replied. "It's a story of incest, isn't it? Doesn't it appeal to the prurient interest?" "No," said Pomeroy. "The average person would be aroused sexually by the idea of two people having sex, but would ignore the mother-and-son aspect. Incest is beyond the average person's scope. The average male doesn't relate to that." Leis was furious at the answer he was getting. To him, the passage was clearly obscene, and no hotshot academic was going to tell him otherwise. He wisely refrained from arguing the fine points of the issue with Pomeroy and just glared his discontent for the benefit of the jury. As he turned his lidded eyes toward his twelve fellow Cincinnatians, you could almost hear him say, "You don't believe this crap, do you?" I wasn't very optimistic. I was worried that the jury, like Leis, would harbor an abiding mistrust—even hostility—toward intellectuals.

Before finishing with Pomeroy, Leis had him read a letter to the editor from a *Hustler* reader in Belleville, Illinois. The reader had praised the July 1975 centerfold, who was portrayed with a cigarette. The model was Althea. The letter had said that "a sexy sensual nude woman with smoke spewing from her nostrils and moist red mouth, with a freshly lit cigarette held between her finely painted fingers, is enough to make me come right now." Leis wanted to introduce the letter as a means of indicting both *Hustler* readers and Althea. He supplemented his cross-examination by introducing into evidence a life-size blowup of Althea's centerfold photo. How the jurors would respond to Althea posing nude was anybody's guess, but the link between Althea and smoking really irked me. We had been planning, as part of the defense strategy, to submit evidence of *Hustler*'s antismoking campaign. With that in mind, I had requested that neither Jimmy nor Althea smoke in view of the press or the jurors. I had given up smoking eight months earlier. Leis had made a preemptive strike.

I thought that *Hustler*'s antismoking campaign was a highlight of my publishing career and an indication of my willingness to engage in an all-out, feisty style of journalism, a style all too lacking in mainstream publications. In the early days of *Hustler* I had sought out cigarette ads in an effort to bring in some needed cash. All the cigarette companies had turned me down. They didn't want to advertise, they said, in such a raunchy magazine. I stewed in quiet for a while, but then became very angry. They were killing hundreds of thousands of people a year selling their carcinogenic product. What evidence was there that pornography did any harm to people? On the contrary, the *President's Report on Obscenity and Pornography* had found no correlation between sex crimes and smut, having concluded that pornography should be made legal to adults. I decided to find a creative outlet for my anger.

Ignoring protests from my advertising director, I had begun running a series of full-page ads on the back cover of *Hustler* showing in graphic detail the effects of smoking. The most memorable were a cancer-ravaged human lung and tongue. No one in a national publication had ever taken on the powerful cigarette companies in such a fearless, uncompromising way. And although I had started it as an attempt to pressure them into placing ads, the antismoking campaign continued when *Hustler*'s circulation began to climb into the millions. A few months before the trial, word had come from the cigarette companies that they were ready to play ball. All they wanted in return was for me to end the antismoking ads. I responded with another back cover ad, this time coupled with an article exposing the deceit and malevolence of the tobacco industry. I was proud of my record and had hoped to present it in court as proof that the magazine was something more than just a porno sheet.

The parade of expert witnesses for my defense continued. It was a wearying routine in which our experts testified that *Hustler* was not appealing to the "prurient interest"—only to be followed by Leis and Cartolano, who would read excerpts out of context into the record in an attempt to paint the most lurid picture possible of the magazine's contents. Leis succeeded in distorting almost everything, including a scatological interview of me in which I was parodying those attributes my critics ascribed to me—not those I actually possessed. Most of those excerpts were read over the objections of Fahringer. Much to Leis's satisfaction, Judge Morrissey allowed almost everything in. When we finally ran out of witnesses, the prosecution brought in its rebuttal team.

Leading off for the prosecution was local TV anchorman Al Schottelkotte. Over the vigorous objections of Fahringer, Schottelkotte was allowed to testify about a poll that his station, WCPO-TV, had conducted. It was a random telephone survey conducted two days before Christmas, involving 470 people. "Forty-seven percent said that magazines which portray explicit sexual acts and nudity in all aspects should be considered legally obscene, 29.4 percent said no, and 23.6 percent were undecided." "I take it you are not a person with special training in opinion taking," Fahringer asked during cross-examination. "No," said Schottelkotte, sitting blank-faced, looking—as Bruce David described him—like a giant turd with clothes on. "Are you aware, Mr. Schottelkotte, that the code of the American Association of Pollsters won't allow them to poll during the two weeks of Christmas or the week before Easter?" "No." Pushing further, Fahringer got Schottelkotte to admit that no attempt had been made to establish the age, race, sex, religion, or occupation of the people called, nor was there any attempt to establish whether or not those surveyed had actually read *Hustler* or any other men's magazine. Finally Fahringer said, "Would you accept my opinion on the value of your television program if I told you I'd never seen it?" "No," Schottelkotte admitted, his voice empty, his expression waning. I looked at the witness stand and—remembering Bruce David's apt description—thought that the turdlike anchorman had just been flushed.

Next up for the prosecution was a bearded young English instructor from the University of Cincinnati, Thomas Sant. Once he took the stand, it quickly became clear that his intellectual image belied a rigid, reactionary, anti-intellectual philosophy. "*Hustler*," Sant said, "has no redeeming literary or artistic value. In fact, the writing is crude and frequently semiliterate. If I were grading this writing in my class, it would average out to a C." "Everybody's a critic," I thought. But as it turned out, Sant's credentials were questionable. He had published no articles or books on pornography (or anything else), was born in Utah to a devout Mormon family, and had lived in Cincinnati for only two years. Speaking softly, Fahringer asked him, "I take it, Mr. Sant, that you have some sympathy for your church's stand against obscenity and other issues?" "Oh, yes," Sant answered. It turned out that he was also against drinking coffee or tea. He hardly reflected Cincinnati's community standards. Pressing on, Fahringer asked Sant, "Do you believe the government has the right to censor literature?" Sant, sensing trouble, fidgeted for a moment. "Yes," he said, "I don't think I should be allowed to read whatever I want. I think the community as a whole should decide; the choice should *not* be left to me." A hush fell over the courtroom. Under Sant's conception of law, freedom of the press would be doomed.

Sant's narrow conception of freedom turned out to be nothing compared to the bizarre opinions of the next witness: Reo Christenson, a political science professor at Miami University in Oxford, Ohio. Christenson was a shriveled, bespectacled academician with the aura of a stern, discipline-oriented Sunday-school teacher. He had taught and written extensively on the subject of pornography and contributed articles to the *Nation, Progressive,* and the *New York Times*. He had also written a section of the minority findings of the *President's Report on Obscenity and Pornography*. Leis had called him in to testify as an authority on Cincinnati's community standards. Christenson started out by stating bluntly that *Hustler* was patently offensive and definitely exceeded local standards of acceptability. In spite of his credentials, I began to suspect his IQ could only be measured in negative integers. During cross-examination the supposed expert on Cincinnati's local standards admitted that he had not gone to a movie or nightclub or read any men's magazines during the past year, and that he had visited the city no more than five or six times. Paul Cambria jumped up and blurted out an objection: "I've been in Cincinnati more days than he has—and I live in New York!" Judge Morrissey, true to form, overruled the objection.

When Cambria's turn to cross-examine the witness came, he opened with the question, "Do you know, Mr. Christenson, that in Hamilton County there are magazines that contain descriptions of incest, bestiality, and which also depict nudity, sexual intercourse, and fellatio?" Christenson got a strange look on his face. "Well," he answered, "yes, but they're not the same, they don't show penises in the anus . . . pulling it out . . . sticking it in the mouth . . . they don't show feces on penises. . . ." I was beginning to wonder what the good Dr. Christenson had been reading. It certainly wasn't *Hustler*. As the witness talked, he began to ramble. Then his eyes started darting around the room, and his head began rhythmically turning side to side. His lips began to curl back against his teeth. It looked as though his mind had snapped. He began to babble and slobber. In a few seconds he had been reduced to a mindless, pathetic man, just a body in a bad suit. "That's it!" I thought. Now I understood what he had in common with Leis, Cartolano, Keating, and the other right-wing, closet perverts who paced the corridors of the Hamilton County Courthouse. They were just suits walking around with bodies in them: empty, incoherent, and blind. While Christenson sat dazed, the lawyers huddled around the judge, speaking quietly. Then the professor was led from the witness stand, confused. The trial had become a circus.

The prosecution's final summation was led by Fred Cartolano, and it presented Fahringer with a bit of a shock. Fahringer's style was to use the same basic summation, with minor tailoring to fit the situation, for all his obscenity cases. And why not? It was a speech he had refined to perfection over the years. Unfortunately, the prosecutors had discovered the secret. As my dapper lawyer sat quietly stricken, Cartolano proceeded to tell the jury exactly what Fahringer intended to say to them. "He will tell you," Cartolano said, "that bringing in a guilty verdict on *Hustler* is comparable to the Salem witch-hunts. He will tell you about the black smoke and the stench of burning flesh from Salem, and he will try to make you believe that it has some relevancy here. He will suggest to you that the witches were burned to protect the children of Salem and that if you, the citizens of Cincinnati, act to prevent your own children from being exposed to this kind of filth, somehow you will be guilty of a similar hysteria. He will tell you that pornography is the witch-hunt of the twentieth century."

As he went on, Cartolano repeated some of Fahringer's signature material—material I had often stolen from him for my own speeches—about freedom being an X-rated movie playing in a nice neighborhood; how a few years ago it was kids with long hair tramping through a federal courthouse, shouting, "Hell no, we won't go!" and how freedom was also construction workers saying, "America, love it or leave it!" "But," Cartolano said, his voice rising, "*Hustler* is EVIL!" The magazine, he argued, could in fact be prosecuted in Hamilton County because it was placed before the public there, "and the law says whoever aids and abets in a crime is just as guilty as the person who actually committed the crime." "*Hustler* will blow your mind," he continued, "because it is the nightmare of a degenerate . . . and don't worry about censorship. That's just the bogeyman all pornographers toss out . . . the law says you have a right to read anything you want in the privacy of your own home. But the law has a right to step in on public distribution. It's not against the law to read or view this kind of material. It is against the law when it is made public to others." It was quite a performance. By the time he was done, I was sick to my stomach.

Fahringer paused after Cartolano finished, appearing to be deep in thought. After a minute he rose, buttoned his suit jacket, and began to speak quietly. "Freedom doesn't mean anything if it's not offensive. Freedom is putting up with an awful lot in society that is distasteful. Freedom is only meaningful if it includes *all* speech, no matter who is offended by it. It would be a hazardous undertaking for anyone to start separating the permissible speech from the impermissible, using the standard of offensiveness. The freedom guaranteed in the First Amendment is indivisible." He stopped and looked back at me. "You can't take it away from Larry Flynt and keep it for yourself. The real issue of this case is: Are we afraid to be free?" I wanted to stand up and cheer, but restrained myself. Fahringer went on to talk about censorship in the Soviet Union, how 85 percent of all the literature condemned there was done so under obscenity statutes. "Watch out, or some day you will find the walls have grown up all around you." As he finished, I could feel tears well up in my eyes. Later Bruce David would ask me, "Are you the hard-nosed prick I work for, or were those tears for the jury?" The tears were real. So were the issues.

Cambria was next. Wearing a dark seersucker suit and horn-rimmed glasses, he waded into the mess with a heavy sense of irony. His voice sounded slightly arrogant, on the verge of being derisive. It was his turn to tell the jury what they could expect to hear from Leis. In a mocking tone, he told the jury to expect Leis to wave a copy of *Hustler* in the air and bellow his displeasure with dramatic indignation. "Oh yes," said Cambria, "I can tell you how the prosecutor will throw those magazines on the floor with an attitude of disgust, and I can tell you how he will then stomp on them to further make his point." As Cambria spoke, I glanced over at Leis. His neck was red. With each revelation the color got brighter. His eyes were radiating hate. Cambria had done his homework. Leis had been nailed, and he knew it. Leis was down, but not out. At the end of Cambria's summation, Leis asked Morrissey to recess court for the day. The jurors, Leis said, needed a rest, even though there was more than ample time to conclude the summation. Morrissey agreed, giving Leis an entire evening to prepare a new summation—which is exactly what he did.

The next morning Leis told the jury, "Sex is a beautiful thing—there's no question about it—but only in the *proper* environment. But these people have taken the beautiful thing of sex and reduced it to the level of an animal. They made love—they made sex—obscene." He then attempted to paint a picture of two lovers running toward each other through an open field, finally locking in a loving embrace. He meant it to be an example of "real" love. Apparently he had seen the depiction on a TV commercial the night before. We all had. His summation was surprisingly short—but certainly not free of drama. As he brought his remarks to a close, he stopped, reached into his pocket, and brought out a piece of chalk. Dramatically bending over, he drew a line across the courtroom floor. "It's time to draw the line against obscenity," he intoned. With that gesture the summation was concluded. All that remained was for the judge to read his charge to the jury, which would then retire to begin deliberations.

There was nothing to do then but wait. And speculate. Which of the jurors were on our side? Which against? Could we count on them? I didn't have many favorable impressions of the faces I had been staring at throughout the trial. We had obtained a *Playboy* subscription list for Hamilton County and knew that two of the jurors were subscribers, although one had lied to the prosecution about it. During the judge's instructions to the jury, Fahringer had bitterly complained to Morrissey about his failure to spell out that they could split the charge—that a guilty verdict on obscenity did not necessitate a conviction on organized crime. Morrissey had refused to elaborate on the charge, stating it was "obvious." But obvious to whom? The jury was not made up of rocket scientists.

The jury began deliberation on a Thursday afternoon. By Friday rumors and leaks led us to believe there was a deadlock. But we couldn't prove it. Despite repeated requests, Morrissey had refused to reveal the nature of the frequent communication between himself and the jurors. I was afraid that Morrissey was applying pressure to the jurors. If the jury was hung, he might be holding them as virtual prisoners in an attempt to force them to a verdict. By the following Monday, communications between the judge and jury increased dramatically. Although we had no way of knowing what was being said, we could keep a record of the buzzer that sounded whenever the jury wanted to contact Morrissey. They were buzzing a lot. We wanted to know the nature of the communications. The judge got cute and said, "Let the record show that the jury buzzed for coffee breaks and for lunch." Fahringer shot back, "The record shows that there are a number of buzzings not accounted for by that." He went on to express his concern that the jurors might feel obligated to bring in a guilty verdict just to be allowed to return to their families. Morrissey interrupted him: "The jurors are having a ball." Fahringer countered, "I don't think it's a pleasant experience." The judge looked down at Fahringer through his reading glasses. "But all through the trial you've been telling us how pleasant *Hustler* magazine is."

The word came back on the following Tuesday afternoon that the jury had reached a verdict. I rushed back to the courtroom with Althea at my side. We sat down with Jimmy and Al at the defense table. The jury filed in, stone-faced, and handed the bailiff the verdict. The bailiff handed the verdict to Morrissey, who read it silently and handed it down to his clerk. The clerk rose, and in the solemn quiet of the Hamilton County Courthouse read the verdict: I was convicted on all charges (pandering, obscenity, and organized crime); Althea, Jimmy, and Al were acquitted. I was stunned. After letting everybody else off, how could they convict me of organized crime and conspiracy? With whom did I conspire?

In most cases there is a delay between conviction and sentencing. But not for me. I was handcuffed immediately and led before the judge. Fahringer pled with Morrissey for a reasonable sentence. Then I requested the opportunity to speak for myself. I was furious. I looked Morrissey in the eye and said, "You haven't made an intelligent decision during the course of this trial, and I don't expect one now." Fahringer was cringing, but I had to say it. Without hesitation, Morrissey pronounced my sentence: $11,000 in fines and seven to twenty-five years in prison—no bond—the maximum sentence. I just stood and blinked, momentarily stunned. Then two bailiffs began pushing me out of the courtroom with a mob of reporters running after me. I shouted at them, "Are we really living in a free country?" I repeated the question, my voice echoing down the courthouse hallway.

7.

Immersed in Boiling Water

JOURNALISTS WHO HAVE COME TO MY OFFICE RECENTLY *have been surprised. They expect a madman or perhaps a crass, foul-mouthed boor. But they find someone else. I am neither mad nor boorish. I don't fit their stereotype— at least not entirely. I can still get angry, it's true, and I like to be outrageous once in a while, but I don't lash out the way I once did. In the past people were anxious to demonize me, and I sometimes gave them reason to do so. I was consumed by anger and ceaselessly intolerant of every form of hypocrisy. I never backed down from a confrontation. I still don't. I will always be intolerant of sanctimonious frauds. But I no longer feel the necessity to push the boundaries quite so hard.*

Don't get me wrong. I still choose to be controversial. Fundamentalists still excoriate me in print. The radical fringe of the feminist movement still calls me "every bit as dangerous as Hitler." But other people aren't so sure anymore. I have a few more allies than I used to. Many feminists now defend pornography. Mainstream journalists feel a certain reluctance to print tired old caricatures of me. Even politicians show a newfound reticence. I'm not used as a straw man quite so often. In the past my name was trotted out in speeches whenever anyone needed a devil figure. But I'm no longer such a convenient scape-goat. People now portray me as melancholy, or weary, or even calm. Yet to use the word calm *in the same sentence with the name* Larry Flynt *seems to many an oxymoron. Yet I am calm, especially compared to years past. And the reason is not hard to understand. I'm not in pain anymore.*

x x x

The bailiffs hustled me down to the Hamilton County Jail as Althea went back to the hotel, distraught and unsure of what was going to happen to me. I wasn't sure, either. As the cell door clanged shut behind me, I stood for a moment, fists clenched, blinking back tears. There was a dirty old derelict in the cell. In a raspy voice he said to me, "Hey, buddy, can you tell me where I can get some justice?" I turned around and smiled at him. "What happened?" I asked him. "I got raped and rolled," he said. Two guys had stolen his welfare check and decided to sodomize him, too. I stared at the guy for a moment. The whole situation seemed fitting in a bizarre sort of way. "When I find the answer," I said, "I'll let you know." Six days later my attorneys filed my appeal and succeeded in getting me out on bond. For the time being I was free. Althea met me at the jailhouse processing center, and we headed back to Bexley, shaken but determined not to let Leis and Keating have the victory.

I wanted Cincinnati, Leis and Keating, and all the city's right-wing fanatics to be the laughingstock of the nation. They deserved to be. They had used their own personal fetishes to define the meaning of what was "obscene" in Cincinnati. To them, sex in general, and the portrayal of it in *Hustler* in particular, was the very definition of "obscene." But the first meaning of the word in my dictionary was "disgusting to the senses," and I did not find sex to be disgusting. I found war and violence to be disgusting, and therefore truly obscene, and had taken my case for an alternative definition to the entire city. It had not made me popular.

In January 1977, a month before the trial, I had mailed a pamphlet to four hundred thousand Cincinnati residents entitled "The Real Obscenity: War." It featured gruesome Vietnam War photos and a questionnaire requesting each resident's view on obscenity. I had promised in a television interview that if a majority of people thought *Hustler* was obscene after having seen the war photos, I would plead guilty to the obscenity charges and serve my time. All hell broke loose. The whole city had been deeply disturbed by the mailing and incensed by the audacity of it. "Who will count the returns?" one reporter asked, openly skeptical of my trustworthiness. I said that my staff would, but offered to take a lie detector test to verify the truthfulness of the count. The poll came out in my favor. I took the lie detector test and passed it. But even though the poll was favorable, the majority of people who had received the mailing were angry and felt that their privacy had been invaded. The pictures had made them uncomfortable, but my point had been made: The obscenity of war could pass through the mail unchallenged, while sex must stand trial. It had made no sense at all. I pondered the irony of it on the way home from jail.

Meanwhile, in the midst of all the legal hassles, my personal life had also been undergoing profound changes. A few months before our arrest on the Cincinnati obscenity charges, Althea and I were driving in my Lincoln. It was a Friday night, the radio was blaring, and I was lost in thought. As I motored along, Althea suddenly turned the volume down and said, "Will you marry me?" I said, "What?" She slid across the seat toward the passenger door, folded her arms, and said, "I think it would show a nice level of commitment." I said, "Why do we need to get married? You know I love you." I didn't want to respond to the "commitment" question. The word *commitment* made me nervous. After a few moments of silence I said, "You know I'm going to sleep with other women, don't you?" She said, "Yes." "And that's not a problem?" I said, querying. "No," she replied. I told her I would think about it and drove on into the night.

On Monday I said yes. My affirmative answer set in motion a flurry of activity. Althea was not one to wait. I bought her an engagement ring right away, and by the end of the week she was already shopping for a wedding dress and had begun to plan every detail of the event. My grandmother and Althea both wanted a church wedding. Althea wasn't religious, but she had the same fantasy most young women do: She wanted to walk down the aisle of a big church, in a beautiful gown, to the strains of the traditional Mendelssohn wedding march. She had a romantic, sentimental streak in her. I agreed to do whatever she wanted, but I wasn't sure any church would want us—or allow us—to use their facility. In fact, no church would. We were turned down by one after another. Just when we thought that no church in Columbus would have us, we got a call from the Reverend Robert F. Sinks, the minister at the Broad Street United Methodist Church, a large downtown congregation. He offered the use of his sanctuary and said he would be glad to conduct the service. I admired his courage—no one else had the nerve to associate with us—and accepted his offer.

On August 21, 1976, at 1:30 in the afternoon, we were married in a traditional service conducted by the Reverend Sinks. Althea's sister, Sherry Maynard, was the matron of honor. Jimmy was my best man. Bob Harrington, the famous "Chaplain of Bourbon Street" in New Orleans, gave the benediction. Harrington had been evangelizing my dancers for years—he was particularly fond of fine-looking women—and was an acquaintance of mine. Althea looked beautiful in her traditional white wedding gown with a long train. I wore a godawful beige tuxedo with wide lapels, the height of fashion in those days of pastel-colored polyester leisure suits. About three hundred and fifty people attended, including family, friends, and a host of magazine wholesalers and industry people. After it was over, Althea and I recessed down the aisle, out the double doors, down the church's steep steps, and into our limousine. We then led a procession of cars to the Bexley mansion, where a catered garden reception awaited the guests. As we arrived at the mansion, the Dick Stein Orchestra struck up a dance tune.

I was thankful that Reverend Sinks was kind enough to let us use his church, and I invited him back to our house for the reception and dinner. He was a middle-aged, ordinary-looking man. Compared to most of the people at the reception, the reverend and his wife looked and acted straight-arrow. But after dinner he cornered me in the living room and began talking in a low, conspiratorial voice. "Larry," he said, "my wife and I would like to hang out and party a little." I said, "Sure, no problem, there's plenty to eat and drink, make yourself at home." He paused for a moment and then said, "Larry, we'd *really* like to party—you know—with, uh, you and Althea." Now I understood what he meant. He wanted to swing with me and Althea. He was hoping for an orgy. I didn't say anything, and let him stand there for a minute. Beads of perspiration were forming on his brow. Finally I said, "You mean, you and your wife want to have sex with us?" He said, "Well, uh, we were thinking . . ." I thought his wife was a cow. I wouldn't have screwed her at gunpoint. "I don't think so," I said, and walked away. I didn't mind him asking, but the hypocrisy did bother me. How could he ask to screw my wife on Saturday and preach the straight-and-narrow on Sunday?

The months following my release from prison were chaotic and full of pressure. My attorneys were preparing the briefs for my appeal, other lawsuits were being filed against me, and the magazine was demanding more and more time and attention. In the midst of this chaos, about seven months after the trial, I found myself catapulted into yet another encounter with organized religion. Althea and I were staying at the Beverly Hills Hotel in California when Joe Wershba, who had produced a "60 Minutes" segment on me, called one morning to say that President Carter's sister, Ruth Carter Stapleton—who had also been the subject of a "60 Minutes" segment—wanted to speak to me. "Why?" I asked him. "Believe it or not," he said, "you two have a lot in common. Like you, Ruth feels that our inability to deal with sexual frustration is rooted in our inability to deal with our religious convictions." At least she's not an ordinary Bible-thumper, I thought. What I couldn't know then was just how extraordinary my encounter with this woman would turn out to be. Wershba gave me her phone number and urged me to call her. With some misgivings, I did.

"This is Larry Flynt," I said into the phone. A soothing voice on the other end said, "This is Ruth Carter Stapleton, and I'm delighted you called. I think we have a lot in common." "That's what Joe Wershba thinks," I said, still skeptical. "Yes," she replied. "We both think sexual repression is bad for people." "Oh," I said, not knowing what to say next. "I want you and Althea to come to dinner at my house," she said. Suddenly I was fumbling for an excuse. "I don't think my schedule will allow it for several weeks," I replied, trying to sound businesslike. "Larry Flynt, you son of a bitch, you know something?" I mumbled, "Er, what?" surprised by her earthiness. "You can do any damn thing you want to," she said—good-naturedly, but with a hint of reproach. As the conversation continued, I ran out of excuses. She was a persuasive lady.

By this time I had my own jet, an Israeli-built Westwind, and on a Friday night a few days later I found myself flying with Althea to Fayetteville, North Carolina, to have dinner with Ruth and Bob, her veterinarian husband. It was truly ironic: We were flying down in my labia-pink jet, a pornographic perquisite, to dine with one of the country's most famous evangelists. Althea was grumpy, communicating her disapproval and wondering out loud why the hell we were going to have dinner with a person with whom we had absolutely nothing in common. I didn't know what to say to her. I wasn't sure why we were going, either.

Ruth and Bob met us at the airport, loaded us into the backseat of their car, and took us to their country club for dinner. Before dinner we sat down in the bar. Ruth and I paired off, and while she drank a club soda and I had a cocktail, she looked at me and said, "Larry, in order to really understand you, and for us to relate, I really need to understand your beginning. Would you tell me all about your life?" She seemed so trustworthy, I just opened up to her, telling her everything I could remember about my childhood and its hardships. At one point I teared up, and as Ruth listened, she began to cry. She was a deeply empathetic person. I found myself attracted to her. After dinner we drove to her house, a modest three-bedroom brick structure, and continued our conversation. Althea and Bob sat together on the living room sofa as Ruth and I spoke. They fell asleep as we talked late into the night.

I told Ruth that I didn't much care for her brother, President Jimmy Carter. She smiled and said, "What *do* you care for?" "Not much of anything," I lied. I cared about many things deeply. "I'm an anarchist," I said. "Jesus was an anarchist," she replied, looking deeply into my eyes with a beautiful, loving, and sexy smile. She then proceeded to tell me about her Jesus and how much she loved him, even confessing that her favorite sexual fantasy was having sex with him. She spoke of Jesus fondly, with deep conviction, admiration, and unselfish devotion. She said that she had committed her life to him, and in the coming months I just might do the same thing. A few days later we continued the conversation when Ruth and Bob spent the weekend with me and Althea at the Bexley mansion. During the visit she asked me if I would help her buy a holistic medicine retreat outside of Denton, Texas, that she intended to name "Holavita." I was charmed by her and said I would help. How could I say no to the first genuine Jesus freak I had ever met? A friendship had begun. I felt genuinely loved by her.

Two weeks later I was called to Los Angeles on business. Ruth was supposed to have a meeting there the same week, so I offered to let her fly with me on my jet. We were the only two passengers. Both of us were in a quiet, pensive mood. I was lost in thought at forty thousand feet, somewhere above the Rockies, when a profound feeling overcame me. I don't know if it was some chemical imbalance in my brain, a symptom of the stress I was under, or a manic-depressive episode. Whatever it was, it was powerful. I suddenly found myself on my knees, praying. I was in the throes of an intense emotional experience. I began talking to the apparition of a bearded figure who suddenly appeared in front of me. The apparition, whom I took to be God, was wearing a white robe and sandals, and a little bearded man was next to him who I thought was the apostle Paul. I was conducting an incoherent dialogue with them about following God and doing the right thing. For some reason—and in retrospect this strikes me as hilarious—comic Lenny Bruce appeared in the vision. I asked God whether Lenny was in heaven or hell. (Sorry, but I can't remember the answer!) And then, in a chilling premonition, I saw myself in a wheelchair. I didn't know what it meant, but it disturbed me deep down in my gut. In a moment Ruth was at my side, holding my hand, hugging me, and speaking soothing words. I felt as though I had been born again. When we arrived in Los Angeles, I was still in the throes of the vision, and Ruth accompanied me to the Beverly Hills Hotel and spent the night with me in my bungalow. No, we didn't do anything sexual. She felt that in my emotional state I shouldn't be left alone. She sat by my bedside and held my hand the whole night through.

The next morning I called Althea to tell her what had happened. I had found God, I told her. I was feeling emotional, and explained to her that I thought I had been representing everything that was wrong with society and that I was ashamed. I cried. Althea listened, at first confused and later angry. "The Lord may have entered your life, but $20 million a year just walked out. Does this mean you'll be pushing dildos *and* crucifixes?" she asked me, dripping sarcasm. Althea neither understood my conversion nor accepted it. For a while she blamed Ruth, and on one occasion she confronted Ruth tearfully, saying, "Give me back my Larry." She was worried that God had become number one in my life and that she had slipped to number two. I had never expected her to feel jealous. I began encouraging her to believe in God, too, but she resisted the pressure as firmly as she had those who had abused her in the orphanages. The nuns, and later the fundamentalist fanatics, had ruined her life and permanently inoculated her against religion. Feeling confused and displaced, she fought depression.

Althea wasn't the only one who thought my conversion was suspect. Those who didn't think I was crazy thought I was dishonest. Most people thought of me as a sybarite, devoted only to money, flesh, comfort, and self-promotion. My conversion was a gimmick to them, just another way for me to increase my publicity quotient and increase profits. I had a reputation for doing things in the extreme and for being a one-man traveling road show. I guess it is fair to say that my born-again experience took on the characteristics of the rest of my life. I didn't just fall for God; I lunged at him, launching into a flurry of new activities.

My thoughts were scattered, but I talked about plans to change *Hustler* into a "Christian magazine." I bought a couple of mainstream journals, including the *Los Angeles Free Press* and the weekly newspaper in Plains, Georgia. I also announced my intention to start a news magazine, to be entitled the *Rebel*.

Meanwhile, as I read the Bible and started associating with a new group of friends, Althea found herself having to talk to me about scripture as much as about magazine copy deadlines. Somehow she managed. Later she would say, "I was never really tempted to become a Christian, mainly because I just couldn't do that to you." She kept an eye on the worldly business of *Hustler* while I pursued a higher calling. And while I was trying to figure out how to work for the Lord, she was trying to guarantee that we stayed in business. *Hustler* was usually put together three months in advance, so there would be no immediate change. But how we would combine religion with a skin magazine was an open question. So while I was reading the prophets, Althea was minding the profits. It made for a very tense relationship.

My conversion also caused chaos at *Hustler*. I decided that my new commitment to women included paying everyone a good wage. At a staff meeting I announced: "Nobody can live on $7,000 a year, so beginning the first of the year, everybody—clerks, editorial assistants, secretaries—will be making a minimum of $15,000 annually. I'm going to turn some of the empty space we've got available into a day care center so women can bring their kids to work and visit them during coffee breaks." My controller thought I was nuts. At another meeting I announced that it was new company policy that smoking was prohibited. People up and down the corridors of *Hustler* were dazed and confused. Some of my employees—presumably those who weren't getting a raise—thought I should see a psychiatrist.

My conversion had even changed my diet. Ruth brought me to religion, but someone else, Dick Gregory, one of my new religious friends, had encouraged me to become a vegetarian. Gregory, the comedian turned social activist, had showed me the advantages of a diet composed of organic carrot juice, mineral water, and high-potency vitamins. In my early years I had lived on a diet of beans and bologna, and when I became successful I ate upscale but still calorie-rich food. After my conversion I lost twenty-five pounds in a matter of weeks. I didn't know it at the time, but my new diet would soon help save my life.

In early 1978, while my appeal of the Cincinnati decision was still pending, another obscenity indictment was filed against *Hustler* in Lawrenceville, Georgia. Even though I had been born again, my stance on the First Amendment had not changed. I decided to fight the new indictment vigorously. I told Ruth about the impending trial, and she offered to accompany me and provide emotional support. I refused to allow her to go, explaining to her that if she did, it would hurt her brother's bid for reelection, and worse, it might damage her ministry. But I appreciated her offer. She was becoming my best friend. The trial was set to begin in the second week of March, so I decided to prepare myself for it by flying to Peter's Island in the Bahamas to spend some time with Dick Gregory. I planned to fast, pray, study my Bible, and try to relax. Ruth thought it was a good idea, although Althea had mixed feelings and decided not to go with me. A week before the trial I returned, refreshed and ready to face the proceedings in Georgia.

Lawrenceville was a quintessential Southern town with a slightly shabby but still dignified courthouse occupying one side of a sun-drenched town square. I entered the courthouse on a Monday morning, March 6. I was accompanied by a team of lawyers, including Paul Cambria, Harold Fahringer's diminutive but feisty partner; and a local attorney, Gene Reeves. The morning proceedings were uneventful, and the judge recessed court for lunch at about eleven. I walked to a local restaurant, the V & J Cafeteria, with my attorneys and had two glasses of grapefruit juice and a little water. We started walking back toward the courthouse about noon, chatting as we went. It was a quiet, peaceful, springlike day.

As we came up the sidewalk to the courthouse steps, it happened. I heard gunshots. "What the hell?" I thought. I turned toward Gene Reeves just in time to see a bullet tear through his arm. He had been shot! As he fell to the ground, I continued to turn in the direction of the sound. Immediately I heard a second shot, but this one hit me. It was like a hot poker had been pushed through my abdomen. As I gasped in pain, I was struck by a second bullet. I looked down and saw that my intestines were spilling out of my body. The first shot had hit at an odd angle and nearly ripped the front of my stomach off. I couldn't tell where the second shot had gone. As my knees buckled and I began to lose consciousness, the first thought that went through my mind was, "Shit! I'm not going to finish the trial today!" It was inconceivable to me that I might die. Then I collapsed face-first on the ground next to Gene and lost consciousness.

An ambulance arrived in less than ten minutes. Somewhere en route to the hospital I regained consciousness, although barely. The attendants were talking to me, saying, "Hang on; we'll be at the hospital in a few minutes." When we arrived at the Gwinnett County Hospital, people were running around and yelling as I was being taken out of the ambulance. A doctor met me as I was wheeled through the door. I looked at him through glassy eyes and said, "Just give me something for the pain, and I'll be all right." I had no idea how serious my injuries were. I had already lost most of my blood from an abdominal artery that had been severed by a .44 Magnum bullet. It was a miracle I was still alive. The doctor didn't answer me, but barked orders to the swarm of nurses and attendants who surrounded my gurney. I was wheeled directly into an operating room.

That country doctor in that tiny hospital did a phenomenal job. He worked for several hours, patching me up the best he could, ignoring the odds and refusing to give up. Within a matter of hours several surgical procedures were performed in a desperate attempt to stop my internal bleeding and repair vital organs. More than six feet of my intestines were removed. My empty bowels temporarily limited the spread of infection. If I had had a full stomach, it would have been much worse. The doctor really didn't think there was much of a chance that I would survive. In fact, he had already told Paul Cambria that I would not make it. Paul told him, "His wife is due here any minute—please don't tell her that!" Paul had called Althea within minutes after I was shot, and she had taken the first commercial flight available. Within three hours, she had arrived at my side.

At some point, after several surgeries had been performed, Althea came in. I was groggy with pain and drugs. We spoke briefly. I said, "They almost got me." Then the doctor asked her to leave, telling her that my spleen had ruptured and there was still internal bleeding they couldn't find. She left in tears. A short time later the beleaguered doctor emerged, saying that he had done all he could, and recommended that I be transferred to the Emory University Hospital in Atlanta by medevac helicopter. Althea gave her consent, and in less than an hour I was flown to Emory.

The first few days at Emory were a blur. A team of doctors performed eleven surgeries on my shattered body to stop the internal bleeding, yet I was still bleeding to death. I was given numerous blood transfusions to replace what I was losing, but in spite of all the operations, no one could find the source of the bleeding. They couldn't continue to transfuse me indefinitely.

The doctors summoned Althea and my family. "He's not going to make it," the doctors informed them. "It's just a matter of time." Althea wept as the doctor promised one last-ditch attempt. I had developed a raging infection by then, but the doctors thought the infection could be controlled. It wouldn't make much difference, though, if I bled to death. My primary physician called his team together for a conference. A young hotshot radiologist had an idea. "I just might be able to find the problem with a CAT scan." It was a relatively new technology at the time. "Why not?" everyone agreed. The doctor ordered several units of blood for me, in the hope that he could increase the bleeding while conducting the CAT scan, thereby improving his chance of spotting the problem.

I was unconscious when they wheeled me into the radiology center and lifted me into the giant machine, but for some reason I woke up in the middle of the procedure. I was nauseated as I regained consciousness, but perked up as I heard the medical staff cheering and laughing. "We found it!" the young radiologist exclaimed. "There is an artery that has been oozing continuously, about one-half inch from your heart. There's a piece of shrapnel in there. A fragment must have nicked it." I celebrated by vomiting blood all over everyone in the room. The doctor took a syringe filled with some sort of sealant, guided it to the leak, and sealed it. My prognosis was temporarily upgraded from "critical" to "poor."

The doctors' optimism about controlling my infection turned out to be unwarranted. Soon after the bleeding was stopped, an abdominal infection began to set in. They flooded me intravenously with several antibiotics, but some stubborn germ had begun to flourish in my gut—one that was immune to every drug in their arsenal. I developed a raging fever, and my abdomen began to swell. In a few hours my stomach was so distended that it looked as though I were pregnant. My prognosis plummeted again. The doctors called my family in once more and told them I had twenty-four to forty-eight hours to live. This dire prediction made the news wire, and in Atlanta a doctor working for the Centers for Disease Control heard it. He called Emory and told them, "We've got a drug that he might respond to. It's not on the market yet—it's still experimental—but we'll make it available to you." My doctor told Althea, who gave her immediate consent and signed a release form. They began dripping the experimental antibiotic into me through an IV catheter as they continued to pack me in ice to prevent brain damage from my fever. Within a few hours the infection began to subside. One more operation drained the infection from my stomach, and I was out of danger. I was going to live—for better or worse.

I had no way of knowing then that for me, the worst had just begun. I couldn't move my legs, even though my spinal cord was intact. A bullet had passed through the bundle of nerves at the base of my spine called the *cauda equina*, Latin for "horse's tail." Instead of severing my spinal cord, which would have left me paralyzed but pain free, the bullet fragments had severed individual nerve fibers, rendering my legs useless but maintaining sensation. I had suffered what was known as "peripheral nerve damage," a type of injury, I soon learned, that was associated with the worst kind of pain. Ironically, as my health improved and full consciousness returned, the pain went up exponentially. With the bleeding stopped and the infection stemmed, only the pain remained. But oh, what pain—unimaginable pain.

No one told me my legs were paralyzed for several days. I was too critical, too weak, and too heavily sedated to comprehend it. But somehow I knew. After I was out of danger, Althea came in to talk to me. Tearfully, she told me the harsh reality of my situation. Fortunately, my genitals and my ability to function sexually were—at least theoretically—unaffected, she told me. I wasn't concerned. I was far too miserable to appreciate the irony of my situation. I understood what she said, but I was so preoccupied with my pain that I didn't care. For the first time in my life I was uninterested in sex. In fact, I wasn't feeling any emotion; I was entirely consumed by the firestorm raging through my body. No one could get an erection while being suspended in a vat of boiling water. And from the time I had regained consciousness, I'd felt as though my lower extremities were immersed in boiling water twenty-four hours a day. The doctors explained to me that the burning sensation I was experiencing was called "causalgia" or "neurogenic pain." I didn't care what the hell they called it; I just wanted relief. But as I soon learned, they could only name the condition, not cure it. Pain, as I came to understand, is elusive, poorly understood, and subjective. The doctors could not see it or measure it; some of them didn't even believe in it. A few thought it was psychological in origin and would go away on its own. They were wrong.

Ruth came to visit me in the hospital, spending hours at my bedside. She would hold my legs and plead with Jesus to make the pain go away. She was an unbelievably compassionate person and seemed to hurt as much as I did. Many of my recent born-again friends wrote me notes. Tammy Faye Bakker sent me a handwritten note on PTL Club letterhead. It said, "The Bible says He allows us to go through the fire that we may become 'as pure gold.'" She had no idea how apt the metaphor was. But I didn't feel like gold; I felt like shit. While a part of me appreciated the sentiment, I couldn't help thinking that no one really understood my predicament. Until you've suffered that kind of pain yourself, you can't understand what it's like. I decided that my physicians were terrible at treating my pain because they hadn't experienced it themselves. They were more concerned with the possibility of my becoming a drug addict than with making me feel better. As I lay there in bed, like some poor, tortured soul in Dante's *Inferno*, the doctors seemed to me nothing more than a bunch of Keystone Kops: running around, bumping into each other, accomplishing nothing. In spite of my ongoing friendship with Ruth Carter Stapleton, my newfound faith was undergoing a slow but sure transformation. I didn't have room for God in my pain-ravaged daily existence, and I began to think that I wasn't particularly interested in the kind of God who would let people suffer as I was.

I spent almost six weeks in the hospital at Emory, and then was transferred to Ohio State University to begin my rehabilitation. But I was restless and didn't want to stay in Columbus. Althea and I had been spending time in Los Angeles before the shooting and were thinking of moving west. I had already taken the preliminary steps to move the *Hustler* offices there. I didn't want to continue my rehabilitation in Columbus and asked my doctors to recommend a hospital in Southern California. They recommended I go to Daniel Freeman Hospital in Inglewood for rehabilitation. I took their suggestion, flew to L.A., and checked into Daniel Freeman.

Although my body was substantially healed, I was nearly insane from the constant, excruciating pain. It was as though I had been disemboweled and hung on a meat hook in my grandpa's smokehouse. I couldn't think about God anymore, or who might have shot me, or anything else. I was utterly consumed by my agony. In Daniel Freeman Hospital the nurses had to change my bedsheets three or four times a day. The pain made me sweat, and I was soaking wet all the time. I cried, screamed, and begged for relief. I took whatever medications they would give me, which was virtually nothing. I spent two months at Daniel Freeman.

Eventually I made the transition in my rehab program to outpatient status and moved into a bungalow at the Beverly Hills Hotel with Althea. She liked living in Los

Angeles, and there were many advantages associated with being in L.A. We decided to sell the Bexley mansion. After a few months at the hotel we leased a house in Beverly Hills from actress Jacqueline Bisset and began to shop for a place to buy. I was very particular but eventually found a place I really liked. It was a Mediterranean mansion that had belonged to a succession of big-name Hollywood stars. It had been built for Errol Flynn, and was later owned by Robert Stack, then Tony Curtis, and most recently by Sonny and Cher. I arranged to have our new estate refurbished and decorated with antiques, and after several months of renovations we moved in and began our new life on the West Coast.

Hustler's move to Los Angeles was good for the magazine. L.A. was less hostile to pornographers and had a much larger talent pool of writers, editors, and art directors than Columbus. It was also a more liberal community, and both Althea and I were weary of the small-minded Ohio conservatives and their constant persecution. In spite of my born-again experience, the magazine had changed little during the months of my recovery. Months before I had run one cover, now infamous, that showed a woman being run through a meat grinder, accompanied by the promise that I would no longer treat a woman like a "piece of meat." It was my flat-footed attempt at apology. No one seemed to understand. But subsequent issues had returned to the old *Hustler* style. By then I was in no shape to make any decisions about editorial content, and Althea did not share my desire to change the magazine's format. *Hustler* had returned to business as usual.

Althea did her best to keep the magazine going and take care of me at the same time. It was a bitter-sweet time. I was in constant agony, always angry, reduced to my animal instincts. I didn't feel like see-ing anybody, much less partying the way I once had. I just wanted to retreat into the dark confines of my bed-room, hunker down, and get through the day. My bed-room became my office. I had a very short attention span, no longer felt like going into the *Hustler* offices, and no longer had any interest in micromanaging the magazine. Before I was shot, I had approved everything that went into print. After the shooting I met with the editors only a couple of times a month. I would accept and reject some material, but I was only doing a little traffic-directing. Althea did the rest. I was relying on her and others to manage the editorial content and maintain the mission of the magazine. She grew thin and highly stressed.

Meanwhile, my full-time obsession was to find a way to deal with the constant burning sensation I felt throughout my body. I became a connoisseur of pain medications. Since I had money, I was able to retain the services of three different doctors, including one in Las Vegas, who would give me prescriptions for what-ever I wanted. Dilaudid was the most powerful pain-killer available. I had plenty of it. I'd give a doctor a couple grand, and the prescriptions would be immedi-ately forthcoming. My bedroom, and the adjoining bath, began to look like a pharmacy storeroom. My nurses were worried about the quantity of heavy-duty drugs I had on hand and refused to give me the doses I wanted. "We'll stay with you and take care of you if you OD," they would say, "and call 911 if we think you need to go to the hospital." But that was all they would do. It didn't matter. I had my own little doctor's bag on the nightstand next to my bed, full of syringes and vials of painkillers. I would draw up a dose, squeeze out the air, and inject myself. It took the edge off, but little else. For a while I was able to get a concoction known as a "Brompton Cocktail." It had been developed for termi- nally ill cancer patients. It was made up of 60 percent morphine, 30 percent pharmaceutical-grade cocaine, and 10 percent alcohol, mixed into a mint-flavored syrup base. The morphine eliminated the pain, and the cocaine kept me awake. One ounce of that stuff and I felt great. For a while I was able to get it through the UCLA pharmacy, until they cut me off, believing that I was taking too much. I found an alternative source for a while, but it dried up, too. The few months I had access to the Brompton Cocktails were the only ones in which I had any relief at all.

I remember Althea taking an informal inventory of the drugs I had on a shelf in the bathroom one night. She said the names out loud as her eyes scanned the rows of boxes. In pill form we had Valium, Percodan, Percocette, Librium, Demerol, morphine, and Dilaudid. Injectable drugs included Valium, Librium, Demerol, morphine, and Dilaudid. We prob- ably had more stuff on hand than the average hospital emergency room. I shot myself up with every single one of them. I overdosed on a regular basis and was taken to the hospital in an ambulance six times. On two of those occasions my heart had stopped, and I was pronounced dead on arrival. But somehow they always managed to revive me. My heart was robust and somehow carried me through. One doctor, after reviving me with a defibrillator, said, "I'm amazed; I've never known anyone with a heart like yours."

Althea soldiered through all these crises, always thinking I would get better. She knew that I couldn't take care of the business and felt a deep sense of responsibility to keep things going. She wasn't relying on drugs to help her cope and didn't have any use for those who did. But as the months, and eventually years, went by, the pressure on her became unbearable. She had listened to me groan and scream around the clock. I wasn't getting better. Somewhere along the line—I'm not sure when—she turned to drugs for respite. The man she loved was like a vegetable. What was there for her to live for?

When Althea had first run *Hustler*, she was exceptionally good at it. No one could have been more effective. She understood our product and our readers. But as her addiction grew, her effectiveness diminished. For a while the drugs didn't make much difference. Drugs don't get to you right away—which was the problem with Althea. She used them recreationally at first and carried on with her duties. But Althea and I had very different personalities and responses to drugs. I don't have an addictive personality, but she did. Some people succumb to drugs and find it impossible to get off them. Althea was one who could not quit. What started out as recreation soon became addiction. At first I didn't realize how bad it was. My mind was always in a fog, distracted by pain and numbed with painkillers. But over a period of months I came to realize the extent of her growing habit. After a while her behavior and appearance were so markedly different that I couldn't miss the change, and I confronted her about it. She admitted the problem, but also let me know she had no intention of stopping.

How could she stop, so long as our bedroom was an addict's paradise? I decided that one concrete step I could take was to put all my pain drugs under lock and key and only give access to the duty nurse. I did, but it made no difference. Althea began to buy street drugs. She hooked up with a couple of pushers who supplied her with cocaine. She didn't always have the cash, but the dealers knew I had plenty of money, and they would give her the goods on credit. I paid a couple of dealers for a while, but then put the word out that I would no longer honor her debts. Finally I had to deal with a couple of dealers in a very harsh way. They left her alone but, like a true addict, Althea found alternative ways to pay. She had a lot of furs and jewels. These began to disappear, most of them before I knew it.

I soon found myself in a very difficult situation. I was immobilized and groggy most of the time, and in no position to give her the attention she needed. In the meantime Althea was making the circuit of Hollywood parties. If you were famous or wealthy in those days, you didn't always need to pay for drugs. They were often free. The town was a drug Mecca, and people gave them away. In the mid-seventies it wasn't unusual for a party to feature a big silver bowl on a central table, filled with a couple of kilos of cocaine. Althea used to go to the Whiskey and Rainbow clubs on Sunset Boulevard, and people would put the stuff in her pocket. It was the wrong town and the wrong environment for someone with an addiction. I didn't know what to do. Beneath the pain, I felt a sense of dread rising deep inside me.

8.
In Contempt

LOOKING BACK, IT IS CLEAR TO ME THAT IN THE
*courtrooms of America the drama of antisexualism has
been repetitiously staged on the issue of pornography.
Prosecutors, judges, and Supreme Court justices have con-
sistently failed in their attempts to differentiate pornography from obscenity. The kind of pornography I publish
is pictorial and subject to interpretation. According to my
critics, the images in* Hustler *are an incitement to sin,
degrading to women, or a threat to "family values." I dis-
agree. I believe that my critics have revealed a great deal
about their own sexual fears and feelings of inadequacy,
but have failed completely in their attempts to differentiate what is truly obscene from what is merely sexual. As
historians have made abundantly clear, this failure is an
inevitable result of a tradition that has considered all
erotic passion sin, even in marriage, and all sexual intercourse a regrettable necessity for procreation. According
to the Simon Leises of this world, women are called to be
saintly and undefiled by the "depravity of the flesh." The*

*idea of sex as playful joy or pure ecstasy is completely for-
eign to them. Consequently, antisexualism has permeat-
ed the halls of Congress, the textbooks of our schools, and
the benches of our courtrooms. Anyone who dares to represent the sexual act or reveal the nakedness of men and
women is to be feared and reviled.*

*The antisexualism of closet perverts like Charles
Keating has a long history. Before his Citizens for Decency
Through Law, there was Anthony Comstock's Committee
for the Suppression of Vice. Comstock managed to get his
extreme antisexualism enacted into law and have himself
appointed a special agent of the Post Office. Until his
death in 1915 he used his position to censor the U.S. mail
for whatever he personally classified as obscene or pornographic. Of pornography Comstock wrote:*

> *The effect of this cursed business on our youth
> and society, no pen can describe. It breeds lust.
> Lust defiles the body, debauches the imagi-
> nation, corrupts the mind, deadens the will,
> destroys the memory, sears the conscience,
> hardens the heart, and damns the soul. It
> unnerves the arm, and steals away the elastic
> step. It robs the soul of manly virtues, and
> imprints upon the mind of the youth, visions
> that throughout life curse the man or woman.
> Like a panorama, the imagination seems to keep
> this hated thing before the mind, until it wears
> its way deeper and deeper, plunging the victim
> into practices that he loathes. This traffic [in
> pornography] has made rakes and libertines in*

society—skeletons in many a household. The family is polluted, the home desecrated, and each generation born into the world is more and more cursed by the inherited weakness, the harvest of this seed-sowing of the Evil One.

Comstock's words are chillingly similar to the rhetoric of those prosecutors and crusaders who have persecuted me over the years. And now the Religious Right has assumed the mantle of Anthony Comstock. The battle is not yet over.

× × ×

The pain following my recovery from the wounds inflicted by my then-unknown assailant was the dominant theme of my private life, but the travails of my public persecution continued in the courts. My personal incapacity did nothing to immunize me from the lawsuits of disgruntled litigants and a host of self-righteous prosecutors out to build their reputations at the expense of the First Amendment. My powers of concentration were poor and my behavior erratic, but somehow I managed to show up for several trials, cause considerable trouble, and in the process make an indelible mark on the history of American jurisprudence. In other words, I continued to be a pain in the ass to those whom I considered hypocrites, stuffed shirts, or assholes.

The appeal of the Cincinnati decision took many months, and while it was pending, I financed an advertising campaign in newspapers around the country. Under the title "Larry Flynt: American Dissident," the ad summarized the facts of the Cincinnati case and said:

> Dissident writers and artists in the Soviet Union and other nations are being vilified and imprisoned, and President Jimmy Carter has stated his deep concern. In the wake of recent events, we urge the President to take a closer look at the restrictions of freedom of expression in America itself. . . . We the undersigned wish to protest the infringement of Mr. Flynt's rights under the First Amendment because it is a threat to the rights of all Americans. We cannot, under any circumstances, approve of government censorship. Further, we urge President Carter and all our fellow citizens to strengthen their commitment to protecting every American's right to freedom of expression.

The document was signed by ninety prominent writers and public figures. Fortunately, when the appeal was finally heard, the decision of Judge Morrissey and the Cincinnati jury was overturned by the appellate court. Unfortunately, it did little to dampen the enthusiasm of other prosecutors. Neither did my shooting garner me any sympathy. I continued to be dragged into court, called to depositions, and solicited for unfriendly interviews. People were unremittingly hostile and would say things like, "Isn't it true, Mr. Flynt, that what you really are is just a smut peddler? What you do is reprehensible! All you want to do is demean women! People have a right in this country not to have your magazine thrown in their face!" It was one derogatory question or statement after another. Everyone felt an obligation to attack me. Their attitude was, "There could be nothing good about what you're doing, so let's just talk about how you're able to get away with it." They all had the same set of preconceived notions.

Before leaving office in 1969, President Lyndon Johnson commissioned a study on obscenity. A blue-ribbon panel of the leading social scientists in the country—and a few others—was made responsible for pulling the report together. Charles Keating was on the panel. (He dissented when it came time to publish the commission's findings.) The commission concluded, after spending $2.6 million dollars and listening to countless experts—social scientists from the major universities and authors who came to testify—that exposure to pornographic materials wasn't harmful to *anyone*. There was simply no evidence of harm. The report concluded that exposure to pornography posed no threat to the adult population. In fact, the original report also concluded that pornography was no threat to children, either. But by the time the commission's report was released, Richard Nixon was president. Nixon said, in effect, "Forget it." And the report has been gathering dust ever since. It was certainly not read by any of the government officials who prosecuted me. In spite of the report, people's preconceived notions were unaltered. They believed what they wanted to.

A curious thing about my ongoing prosecutions was the fact that *Playboy* and *Penthouse* were exempted from the same kind of animus. Their respective publishers, Hugh Hefner and Bob Guccione, always tried to masquerade their pornography as art and justify it by including articles that were supposed to have had so-called "redeeming social value." But as transparent as the strategy was, it worked. I knew Hefner and Guccione and was taken with the fact that both of them were very uncomfortable with what they were doing. They wanted to be looked at as respected, important publishers. That was fine with me. I liked Hefner and still consider him a friend. "You can be respected," I thought, "and important. But you *still* publish pornography. Acknowledge it, be proud of it, or get out of the business." I hate pretentiousness—even among fellow pornographers.

My dislike for the pretensions of *Penthouse* publisher Bob Guccione and his girlfriend *du jour* in 1976, Kathy Keeton, landed me in court. Guccione had sued me, claiming I had libeled him by printing a cartoon in *Hustler* that suggested he engaged in homosexual activity. Keeton filed suit because I had printed a cartoon suggesting she had contracted VD from Guccione. The Keeton cartoon had run in the May 1976 issue of *Hustler*, but the case was not tried until June 1979. The Guccione case was heard in Ohio, and I lost—big time. A judgment of $39.6 million was levied against *Hustler* and me, but it was later reversed on appeal. Keeton tried to file a belated case of her own in New Hampshire after the Guccione case was overturned.

Why there? The statute of limitations had expired, and she couldn't file in any other state. New Hampshire had a six-year statute, the longest in the country. Of course, she had never set foot in New Hampshire, and *Hustler* did not have offices there; but the magazine was sold in the state, and her attorneys used that fact as a pretext for bringing a claim. Unfortunately for Ms. Keeton, the New Hampshire District Court dismissed her case, stating that it had no jurisdiction. She appealed the dismissal in federal court, which upheld the state court's decision. She then pushed the case all the way up to the Supreme Court.

At first—in my pain-filled, reclusive state of mind—I decided to let my attorneys deal with the matter. I hired a woman to help represent me, a law professor who specialized in Supreme Court cases and jurisdictional issues. But I later decided to represent myself, and having heard this, she quit several weeks before the case was due to be heard. The legal principle at stake in the case was simple, and even in my drug-induced stupor I was capable of delineating it. I wrote the court and notified it of my intention. The court had already determined that mentally competent criminal defendants had the right to represent themselves, so why couldn't a civil litigant do the same thing? I certainly had not been certified as mentally incompetent. The court ignored my letter and appointed an attorney from Chicago whom I did not know. "How can they do this?" I thought.

When the day of the hearing arrived, I traveled to Washington, D.C., with a large entourage, expecting to represent myself. I gave notice to the clerk before the hearing, notifying the justices that I was in the audience and expected to be heard. I got no response. Keeton's attorney, and then the attorney the court had appointed for me, were both invited to present their arguments. After they were done, Chief Justice Burger adjourned the proceeding. I thought my rights had been trampled on and was furious. As the justices rose, looking like nine solemn priests in their judicial vestments, my anger overtook me. I shouted from the audience, "You're nothing but eight assholes and a token cunt!" Burger turned around, pointed at me, and said, "Arrest that man!" As I was wheeled out of the courtroom, a bailiff placed me under arrest and took me to a small room right outside the main courtroom. It was clear that the bailiff was improvising. They didn't have a booking room or a holding cell.

In fact, no one could remember anyone ever having been arrested for contempt before, much less for using language so colorful. I was booked for disruption of the Supreme Court by a bailiff who had never been required—in his entire career—to exercise such a duty. He was plainly amused. He took me downstairs to a holding cell, where another bailiff decided that he should fingerprint me, and proceeded to do so. Holding up my hand and looking at my ink-stained fingers, I quipped to the bailiff, "Once these fingerprints are in the system, I'll never be able to get work in this town." The bailiff, with a wry grin on his face, replied, "Funny how things get lost around here," and dropped the fingerprint card in the trash can.

By this time I had an urgent need to find a bathroom. But, as I soon discovered, the Supreme Court had no handicapped bathrooms. The bailiffs talked it over and decided the only thing they could do was take me to a local hospital so I could use the toilet. From there they would take me to my arraignment across town. But the logistics were becoming difficult. The Supreme Court has its own police force, with jurisdiction over the one square block occupied by the courthouse itself. They didn't have a paddy wagon or patrol cars or any other means of transportation. They were going to have to rely on the District of Columbia police to transport me. A call was made, and a bailiff took me downstairs in an elevator and wheeled me to an underground driveway. In a few minutes a D.C. police van showed up. A heated discussion ensued. The D.C. cops, not having realized I was in a wheelchair, did not want to transport me. They were afraid I would roll around in the van and be injured. They refused to take me. A D.C. police officer said, "I'm not taking responsibility for this." Another said, "It's your arrest; you handle it!"

Ever the improviser, I quickly formulated a solution. Why not put me in my own limousine with a police chaperone and transport me to jail in *style*? I called the sergeant over and explained my plan to him. An agreement was promptly worked out. The limo was summoned. In fact, several limos were summoned. My entourage had arrived in a caravan of stretch limousines. My own limo, festooned with American flags on the front fenders, soon replaced the police van in the driveway. The cops took one look at the flags and said,

"No way! [According to tradition, only the vehicles of heads of state and high-ranking officials could bear flags.] You've got to take the flags off," they said. "Why?" I replied. "There's no law against having American flags on your car." They argued with me for a minute, walked over, removed the flags, broke them, and left. Like a good Boy Scout, however, I was prepared. Two spare flags were in the trunk. I had the driver retrieve them and install them in the limo's flag holders. I was placed inside by two other policemen. They didn't care about the flags. The two amused cops then joined me in the backseat, one on each side. And so the parade left the courthouse. Led by a police escort, the line of limos cut across town to the hospital with my limo leading the way, flags flying.

The limo went directly to the emergency room entrance, with all the others right behind it. The medical staff came out gawking, thinking there was some kind of crisis. Looking at the American flags, a nurse said, "Was the President shot?" The cop replied, "No, we have a prisoner who needs to use the bathroom." The nurse thought the cop was nuts. "You can't be serious," she said. "We're serious," he replied. The two cops rolled me through the entrance and down the hall to a bathroom. After I had relieved myself, they put me back in the limo, and we drove to the local courthouse.

Once we got there, I was taken downstairs to a holding cell. While I was still in the car, I had taken off my dress shirt to expose a T-shirt I had made for the benefit of the Supreme Court justices. Across the front, in block letters, it read, FUCK THIS COURT. The holding area of the court building was run by a bunch of big, burly marshals with buzz cuts and a lot of attitude. They didn't like my shirt very much. They told me, "You gotta take that shirt off." I said, "Bullshit!" They said, "Either you take it off or we'll take it off you." I said, "I have a right to wear this shirt." I let them know they were going to have to physically attack me—in my wheelchair—if they wanted that shirt off. I guess they thought their macho image would be tarnished if they wrestled it off me. They didn't do anything. We argued back and forth for a while, and I finally agreed to put a jacket over the T-shirt. After I did, they wheeled me upstairs to the courtroom. Of course, as soon as I got there, I took the jacket off.

The judge for my arraignment was a nice woman and an unflappable jurist. The marshals were fuming on the sidelines, a crimson flush coloring their necks and faces. I grinned at them. The judge looked slightly amused, but did not react to my shirt. She read the charges, set bail—which was immediately posted—banged the gavel, and went on to the next case. Within an hour I was free. When I got back to California, my lawyers had the case moved to the West Coast. The Justice Department tried to act tough for a few weeks, but my attorney, Alan Isaacman, told them we were prepared to go to trial. "You'll want to know," he told the government lawyers, "that we're subpoenaing all the Supreme Court justices." "You can't do that!" they said. "They're too busy!" "Oh, yes, we can," replied Isaacman. "Every defendant has the right to face his accusers." In the end the charges were dismissed. And a few months later the Supreme Court ruled partially in my favor. Kathy Keeton's case was sent back to state court, where it languished for years.

In the months prior to the Supreme Court debacle over the Keeton case, John DeLorean and his eponymous car company had been making the national news. In my life as a recluse, I had been following the DeLorean story on the television in my bedroom. Over the years, I have received many photographs and videotapes of the rich, famous, and infamous *in flagrante delicto*. Some people consider me the hypocrisy police, and when they find or have access to blackmail-worthy material, they send it to me. I never blackmail people, but I don't mind exposing frauds. I've published a few compromising photos in *Hustler* and have destroyed many more. I don't deliberately try to hurt innocent people. I've received embarrassing, sexually explicit images of Pat Boone, Ted Turner and Jane Fonda, Pamela Lee Anderson, and several right-wing politicians. But until John DeLorean, I had never caught the federal government with its pants down.

DeLorean had been arrested by the FBI for possession of cocaine—a large quantity of it—that he was allegedly going to sell in the hopes of bailing out his failing car company. DeLorean, whose sports car was a marketing disaster clad in brushed stainless steel, was on the brink of bankruptcy. DeLorean had been desperately seeking ways to recoup his debt and had been arrested in the process. One day, after newscasts had broadcast the story, I received an unsolicited package from an anonymous clerk in the offices of DeLorean's defense attorneys. The package contained a videotape of the arrest and the events immediately preceding it. It was a bombshell, showing how the FBI agents had entrapped the desperate entrepreneur. After viewing the tape, I decided that it should be seen by a national audience. The idea of our government entrapping people—luring them into crime and then arresting them—really upset me. Without the FBI's involvement there would have been no crime. Its agent both supplied the cocaine and suggested that its sale was the answer to DeLorean's problems.

Don Hewitt, the Emmy-winning producer of "60 Minutes" I'd met years earlier, had received a tip that I had some very interesting tapes. He called one morning from New York and asked if he could see me immediately. "Come on out," I said. Several hours later he arrived. Althea let him in and ushered him into my den. The tape was already loaded in the VCR, and I was sitting in front of the television, fingering the remote control. "Let's see it," Hewitt said, skipping the small talk. I punched the button, and the black-and-white surveillance tape started playing. When it was done, Hewitt cried, "Jesus Christ! How the hell did you get that?" "I never reveal my sources," I said, grinning.

Word leaked that "60 Minutes" had the tape, and within a few days federal prosecutors, DeLorean's attorneys, and lawyers for CBS were in court. The feds wanted an injunction barring the network from broadcasting the tape. None was issued, and the tape aired the following Sunday. It caused a sensation.

Newspapers trumpeted the headlines: "DeLorean Trial Postponed Indefinitely"; "DeLorean Attorneys Ask for Dismissal of All Charges"; "Flynt Tape Destroys Trial." I thought the tape was an indictment of the federal government and not DeLorean and was glad to see the whole matter put on hold. But it was not on hold for long. The feds brought the case to trial a short time later, hoping that the furor over the videotape had died down sufficiently to resume trial proceedings. Perhaps it had, but in the meantime I had been working my sources and come into possession of *another* tape, this time an audio recording. I called a press conference on the lawn of my estate to reveal its contents.

The scratchy, barely audible recording was difficult to understand, so I had prepared a transcript to hand out. I first played the tape into a microphone. Everyone strained to hear. The reporters could make out what sounded like DeLorean's voice speaking in plaintive tones to another man, presumably a federal agent. The transcript filled in the blanks for them. On the tape DeLorean pleaded to be let out of the cocaine deal, but the agent threatened to harm his daughter if he pulled out. It was inflammatory material. I could not authenticate the tape, but had every reason to believe it was real. And if it was, the federal case was in shambles.

The unruly crowd of reporters went crazy. They milled around me as my bodyguards nervously tried to keep order. "Play it again," several people shouted. "Okay," I said. It wasn't any more audible the second time around. By this time I was encircled by reporters.

Some were asking questions, others joking. One of them said, "Mr. Flynt, how about a tour of the house?" I said, "Sure, why not?" Distracted, I had my bodyguard wheel me into the house with a crowd of reporters following. I left the tape and player outside. I didn't even think about it until later in the day. I sent an aide out to bring it inside. It was nowhere to be found. To this day people are skeptical of the tape's sudden loss. I don't know what to tell them. It really was lost. Obviously someone took it, but at the time it seemed as though it had vanished into thin air.

Robert Takasugi, the judge assigned to the De-Lorean case, thought I was out to ruin the trial and issued a subpoena ordering me to appear in court with the audiotape. I was in a foul mood and decided not to cooperate. Takasugi issued a warrant for my arrest, and on November 1, 1983—my forty-first birthday—a squad of fifteen federal marshals arrested me at my house and hauled me into the presence of a stern Robert Takasugi. He demanded the tape. I told him it was lost. He reluctantly agreed to believe me. He then asked, "Who was the source of your audiotape?" I didn't feel like answering the question. It seemed insolent to me. No one had a right to ask a publisher or journalist about his confidential sources. I began to ramble, talking about other tapes that had come into my possession, not answering his question. "What does this have to do with the DeLorean tape?" Takasugi boomed, his patience having run out. "Oh nothing, Your Honor," I replied. After a few more brief exchanges, Takasugi announced that he was going to fine me $10,000 a day until I revealed my source. He ordered me back the following day and banged down the gavel.

My FUCK THIS COURT T-shirt was a hard act to follow, but I managed to come up with something even more outrageous for my next day's court appearance before his honor, Judge Takasugi. I was angry, in terrible pain, and loaded up on painkillers. It was a potent combination. Annie Liebowitz was at my house, preparing to photograph me for *Vanity Fair* magazine. She had me carefully posed—nude, on a couch with an American flag—when Alan Isaacman called and told me I had to be in Takasugi's court in one hour. I thought to myself, "I'm being summoned to court like a naughty child, so I might as well act like one." I took the flag that Annie had brought, and asked my nurse to pin it on me, like a diaper. I wore it to court. Takasugi asked me a few questions, ordered me not to leave the state, and told me I was to make myself available to the court at all times. Takasugi said nothing to me about the flag, but the hardass federal prosecutor had me arrested outside the courtroom by the marshal for desecrating Old Glory.

Two weeks later I was arraigned on the flag desecration charge before a federal magistrate. The pain was unbearable that day. I needed a dose of something, but I was going to have to wait until I got home. When Magistrate McMahon finally got around to my case, I couldn't hold my anger in any longer. We got into a heated argument. McMahon ordered me to undergo a psychiatric examination. He did not, however, charge me with contempt. Unfortunately, a senior judge heard about the noisy confrontation and ordered me to appear at another hearing, where I was to "show cause" why I should not be charged with contempt. A month later, on the appointed day, I showed up for the hearing—but I was in no mood to be browbeaten by some judge.

I was wheeled into the courtroom of the surly federal jurist Manuel Real. Real had a bad reputation and a short temper. The two of us were a volatile mixture. Real confronted me with stern words about my behavior with the flag. A nasty exchange ensued. I wasn't making much sense and was only able to communicate anger. And it was intense. I had much to be enraged about. My life was a fucking mess, and my words reflected my feelings. Real told me to watch my language. At one point I became so enraged that I spit at him. He screamed at the bailiff, "Gag that man!" The bailiff found some tape and covered my mouth. Real continued to question me, but now I could only shake my head to indicate yes or no. After receiving my assurance that I would act civilly, he ordered the bailiff to remove the tape. I wasn't civil and shouted several obscenities. Real exploded in anger. "Mr. Flynt!" he shouted. "I'm sentencing you to six months in a federal psychiatric prison! Now get out of my courtroom!" I screamed at him, "Motherfucker—is that the best you can do?" He shouted back, "No! I'm making that twelve months!" I shouted again, "Listen, motherfucker, is *that* the best you can do?" He rose from his chair and stormed off the bench into his chambers. As he went, he said, "Fifteen months!" The bailiff wheeled me away. Within an hour I was at the federal prison on Terminal Island.

Nineteen eighty-three was an eventful year in many ways. A few months before my run-in with Real, I had met with a renowned neurosurgeon named Milton Heifitz. Heifitz had developed some pioneering techniques for dealing with brain aneurysms and other previously untreatable conditions. I went to see him because the effectiveness of my pain medications was decreasing over time. He told me that he was a "head man," not a "back man." "But," he told me, "you ought to see Blaine Nashold at the Duke University Medical Center. He's developed a new technique for dealing with nerve pain." I called Duke immediately and made an appointment. Nashold told me that he and a team of other physicians at the university were using a new technique that involved the precision cauterization of individual nerve fibers with a laser. They were experimenting with a process in which individual fibers were teased out of a nerve bundle and then severed by the laser with great precision. The technique offered the hope of eliminating my pain without damaging adjacent nerves, which would allow me to maintain control of my bladder and bowel functions.

After the consultation I scheduled the first available surgery date with Dr. Nashold and had the procedure performed a few weeks later. It was only partially successful. The doctors were understandably conservative in their use of the laser, and not all of the nerves responsible for my pain were cauterized. But I did feel better. I would say that the operation reduced my pain level about one half. The sensation in my legs went from feeling as though I had been immersed in boiling water to feeling that I was immersed in scalding water—better, admittedly, but not much. Offsetting this gain was the fact that the effectiveness of my pain medicine continued its steady decline. However, I took the partial success of the surgery to be a good sign that future gains might be possible. It was the first ray of light I had seen since the shooting. It energized me for a while.

Shortly after my surgery at Duke, but before my run-in with Judge Real, I began an operation of my own—one intended to promote the sales of *Hustler*. I decided to run for president. It was a tongue-in-cheek campaign, but not everyone realized it. I had started a newsmagazine—as I had planned to do after my short-lived conversion—but it was hardly the mainstream publication I had envisioned while under the influence of my born-again experience. The *Rebel* was the most irreverent newsmagazine in the country and served as my bully pulpit. I used it to announce my presidential candidacy. On the editorial page of the December 31, 1983, issue a picture appeared showing me wearing a LARRY FLYNT FOR PRESIDENT T-shirt. Below the picture was the question "Who will be our next president?" The opening sentences of my editorial set the tone:

> It is now obvious to the world that the nuclear-mad cowboy, Ronnie Reagan, and

his entire cabinet must resign in disgrace. Reagangate, as I have penned it, is a scandal that could never have happened [before] in the history of the world because never has this planet ever had such a dumb fascist bigoted motherfucker as a world leader.

I wrote those words while in solitary confinement at the Federal Prison Medical Center in Springfield, Missouri, courtesy of Judge Real. I also said in the editorial that perhaps Reagan and his cabinet could join me at Springfield for a complete psychiatric evaluation. "Maybe the prison shrink, Dr. Logan, will have some answers for the American people. . . ." I added, "God knows we need them."

In addition to garnering publicity for *Hustler*, my farcical presidential campaign tested some real issues. I had a compulsion to find the loopholes in the nation's obscenity laws. I knew that the equal-time provision of the Federal Communications Act prohibited censorship of any ad in which a candidate's voice or picture appeared, while the U.S. Criminal Code banned the dissemination of obscene material. I prepared an X-rated television commercial that included both my picture and my voice. I sent it to several television stations, insisting that it be shown. The station managers nearly passed out at the prospect of airing my ads and refused to broadcast them. I forced the Federal Communications Commission (FCC) to issue an opinion. It ruled against my ads, but only after I had caused much consternation in the halls of government—and had a helluva good time doing it. The FCC certainly took my presidential campaign seriously, and, amazingly, so did many citizens. I received hundreds of donations—an unexpected measure of the dissatisfaction that many ordinary people felt with the Reagan Administration.

In addition to the editorials I wrote for the *Rebel* during my incarceration, I also managed to engage in other publicity-generating activities. My experience in federal prison was certainly hellish, but it was not unproductive. I was sent to two different correctional facilities: Springfield, Missouri, and Butner, North Carolina. At both I did my best to make life miserable for those who had confined me, and at the same time I kept my publicity machine going. Most people who go into the federal prison system are isolated and powerless. I wasn't. I had a whole team of attorneys monitoring my treatment, and a host of reporters and journalists clamoring for news about my condition. I released regular statements from my cell about my presidential campaign, the DeLorean case, and other issues I was exploiting. I found the whole situation easy to manipulate and used my incarceration in every creative way I could. The feds never managed to isolate me. I'd call my office, for instance, and have them patch me through to CNN in Atlanta for an interview. It really pissed off the authorities, but they couldn't stop me.

The federal prison system just wasn't able to control a determined asshole like me. The wardens told my brother, Jimmy, on several occasions that they wished they could get rid of me. "He's destroying our life," they would say. I had no patience for their simpleminded technologies of control. While I was in Butner, they tried out a new behavior modification technique on me. It was a system of rewards and punishments appropriate for a child or an idiot, but not an adult man. When I refused to obey them, or engaged in some "inappropriate behavior," they would penalize me by taking away my radio or some other basic privilege. Naturally, I did not cooperate in *any* way and soon found myself devoid of all perks and privileges. A paternalistic shrink would come into my cell, scold me like a child, and then hold out the hope of reward. They thought they could train me like some chimpanzee. That kind of treatment only succeeded in motivating my basest instincts. One day when the shrink came in, I threw my own feces at him. It was a direct hit. I shouted at him, "You motherfucker, you took everything away from me, but you can't take my heart!" Faced with the failure of their behavior-mod technique, they were glad to get rid of me.

The Springfield prison had been anxious to get rid of me, too. I had drawn too much attention to the institution, and publicity was something the system did not like. Butner had been the unwilling heir of my troublemaking presence. The warden at Butner knew full well why I had been transferred from Springfield. The federal prison system is a small fraternity of administrators and wardens. I had left a trail that extended back through Springfield to Terminal Island in California. My presence at Springfield had nearly cost its Warden Pataski his job. Althea came to visit me regularly, and on one occasion she met the warden's daughter, Lisa. Althea and Lisa got to know each other, and after a while they began to party together. They smoked a little dope and snorted a few lines of coke. The word got out that Althea had involved the warden's daughter in drugs. Lisa Pataski had been doing drugs for a long time, but had previously managed to conceal her involvement. But after her habit was revealed, and in light of the rumors about Althea's role in it, the feds decided that if Pataski could not control his daughter, he could not control a major prison, either. Pataski was transferred to the boondocks after I was sent to Butner. Five and one-half months later, I was released. The Ninth Circuit Court had overruled Real and dismissed the contempt charges.

My presidential candidacy was short-lived, and a few weeks after I was released from Butner, I folded the campaign. My candidacy had served its purpose, garnering much publicity for *Hustler* and drawing attention to several political and social issues I cared about. In the spirit of my new civic involvement, and with tongue firmly in cheek, I decided to continue to enlighten members of the U.S. Congress and Senate on a regular basis. I was no longer making speeches, so the logical medium for this enlightenment was *Hustler* magazine. I sent a free subscription to every member of Congress, every senator, and all nine justices of the Supreme Court. In a press release I said that the free subscription would help them be "well informed on all social issues and trends." I also thought it might give some of the old farts the first erection they had had in years. The conservatives in the House and Senate had a fit and ordered the Post Office to ban delivery of *Hustler* to them. I filed suit and blocked the ban in federal court. The issue was eventually settled when a judge ruled that it would be unconstitutional to enforce such a ban. While the case was pending—and *Hustler* was still being delivered—I decided to have some fun with the senate's biggest bigot: Jesse Helms. In the back of *Hustler*, where all the sex ads were located, I had my art department design a phone-sex advertisement for Jesse. At the top of the ad it said: "JESSE HELMS—PHONE SEX—BLACKS PREFERRED." We included his office telephone number and his number on the Senate floor. Then we added at the bottom, "If no answer, call . . ." Also printed was his home number, which we had acquired from a reporter. Helms received so many calls that he had to disconnect his home phone. Too bad.

9.
A Highly Flexible Morality

THE MAINSTREAM PRESS HAS NEVER BEEN FRIENDLY
to me, and at times it has been openly hostile. Yet some of
the most important court cases affecting freedom of the
press—cases in which I was a litigant—have been treated
only as ordinary news stories. The press has been much
more interested in my antics than in my principles.
Nevertheless, it has been my principles that have motivated me, and in the end those principles have protected
their freedoms. The indifference of the mainstream press,
however, has not been shared by academics. Like me or
not, I have made a difference. There is an increasingly
large body of literature written about Hustler and me by
feminists, critics, and social historians. One of them,
Laura Kipnis, has written: "The very public nature of
Flynt's blazing trail through the civil and criminal justice
system and his one-man campaign for the First Amendment justify [our] interest . . . because Flynt himself has
had a decisive historical and political impact on the
realpolitik of state power. In the end it has been porn king

Larry Flynt—not the left, not the avant garde—who has decisively expanded the perimeters of free speech." Why has the mainstream press been so reluctant to weigh in on the side of freedom of expression? This is a question every reporter and journalist needs to ask—and answer—for himself.

x x x

In November 1983—the same month that I was held in contempt by the Supreme Court at the Keeton hearing, and the same month I had been consigned to federal prison for my run-in with Judge Manuel Real—*Hustler* ran an ad parody on the inside of its front cover lampooning a person I considered to be one of America's biggest hypocrites: the leader of the so-called "Moral Majority," Jerry Falwell. I didn't know it at the time, but the Falwell parody initiated a process that would wind through the courts for almost five years and eventually end in a landmark decision by the Supreme Court of the United States. It would become the most important legal battle of my publishing career.

It all began with an advertisement by the Italian liquor company Campari, which ran a major advertising campaign in mainstream magazines, including *Cosmopolitan*, *Vogue*, and the *New Yorker*, from 1981 to 1983. To entice consumers to try Campari, a Madison Avenue ad agency had designed a series of high-class magazine layouts in which celebrities talked about the "first time" they had tasted the liqueur, with an obvious sexual *double entendre*. With elegant typography, spare copy, and carefully composed photos, the claim was subtly made that Campari, like sex, got better after the "first time." The version of the ad that ran in *Hustler*, however, was more single *entendre*. Against the backdrop of a Campari bottle, a glass of Campari on the rocks, and a picture of Falwell, was the headline, "Jerry Falwell Talks About His First Time." An "interview" with Falwell followed:

FALWELL: My first time was in an outhouse outside Lynchburg, Virginia.

INTERVIEWER: Wasn't it a little cramped?

FALWELL: Not after I kicked the goat out.

INTERVIEWER: I see. You must tell me all about it.

FALWELL: I never *really* expected to make it with Mom, but then after she showed all the other guys in town such a good time, I figured, "What the hell!"

INTERVIEWER: But your Mom? Isn't that a bit odd?

FALWELL: I don't think so. Looks don't mean that much to me in a woman.

INTERVIEWER: Go on.

FALWELL: Well, we were drunk off our God-fearing asses on Campari, ginger ale and soda—that's called a Fire and Brimstone—at the time. And Mom looked better than a Baptist whore with a $100 donation.

INTERVIEWER: Campari in the crapper with Mom . . . how interesting. Well, how was it?

FALWELL: The Campari was great, but Mom passed out before I could come.

INTERVIEWER: Did you ever try it again?

FALWELL: Sure . . . lots of times. But not in the outhouse. Between Mom and the shit, the flies were too much to bear.

INTERVIEWER: We meant the Campari.

FALWELL: Oh, yeah. I always get sloshed before I go out to the pulpit. You don't think I could lay down all that bullshit sober, do you?

At the bottom of the ad, in small print, were the words "Ad parody—Not to be taken seriously."

A few days after the issue was released, Falwell was leaving a Washington, D.C., news conference when a reporter held up a copy of the November *Hustler* and shouted, "Reverend Falwell, have you seen this?" He hadn't, but when he got back to Lynchburg, Virginia— his headquarters—he sent an aide to a local newsstand to buy a copy. He would later say that he was "stunned" to see his image on what appeared to be a celebrity endorsement of a liquor product. But not nearly as stunned as when he read the accompanying text. Although the disclaimer said, "Not to be taken seriously," Falwell took it *very* seriously. "I have never been as angry as I was at that moment," he said. The preacher added that he "felt like weeping," but instead he decided to file a $45 million lawsuit against me and *Hustler*. He also consoled his hurt feelings with a major fundraising campaign, allegedly to help defray his legal expenses, reprinting the Campari ad and mailing it to one million of his "Prayer Partners." In return they sent him more than $700,000—a considerable war chest.

The Falwell lawsuit incorporated many ironies, not the least of which was his choice of counsel. He selected one of the most colorful attorneys in America, Norman Roy Grutman, of the New York firm Grutman, Miller, Greenspoon, Hendler, and Levin. Grutman was the longtime lawyer for Bob Guccione and *Penthouse* magazine—a fact well known to Falwell. Falwell's income—raised from little old ladies and major donors from the Bible Belt—was going to be paid to a lawyer who had made a fortune defending pornographers. As one observer put it, it was the "Baptist-to-*Penthouse*" equivalent of the "Iran-Contra" connection. Few, if any, of Falwell's small donors knew that the ultimate destination of their hard-earned cash was the bank account of Norman Roy Grutman.

Grutman was a pompous upper-crust New York litigator. He had gone to an exclusive prep school, attended college at Yale, and finished his law degree at Columbia. His credentials were impeccable, but his reputation among other lawyers was terrible. He had a reputation for ruthlessness. He would do anything to win, had absolutely no compassion for anyone, and in the opinion of many, had no ethical constraints on his behavior whatsoever. Opposing lawyers believed that he had paid witnesses to lie, that he enjoyed bullying people who were in poor health, and that he was rude and offensive in every encounter. My attorney received calls from lawyers all around the country who had opposed him in court, complaining that Grutman was a low-life, no-good sonofabitch. There was even an informal group of lawyers who considered themselves the "Anti-Grutman Club."

But Grutman's reputation, and his association with *Penthouse*, did not bother Falwell in the least. Falwell apparently saw no moral contradiction in retaining a lawyer with such an unsavory character. Grutman, in addition to having represented *Penthouse*—a magazine that had previously earned Falwell's hearty condemnation—had also been reprimanded by the courts numerous times for his lack of personal and professional integrity. And now he was representing an organization whose very name suggested moral superiority. In previous cases Grutman had been cited by judges for, among other things, having "flagrantly and deliberately misconducted [himself] in reprehensible manners which were calculated to improperly prejudice plaintiffs and improperly influence the jury against plaintiffs." In another case a judge had said about Grutman, "[His] defiance climaxed a sordid pattern of prolonged and vexatious destruction of legitimate discovery; [this pattern] included false testimony [and] material misrepresentations by counsel." In spite of these profound ironies, Falwell's choice of Grutman made nary a ripple in the mainstream press, in spite of the fact that his "end justifies the means" ethics were a complete contradiction of what he espoused in the pulpit.

One more irony: Jerry Falwell had severely criticized President Jimmy Carter for an interview that appeared in *Playboy* magazine. Some months later a freelance reporter had interviewed Falwell "at large." The interview was sold to the highest bidder and published—in *Penthouse*. Falwell filed suit against *Penthouse*. The case was thrown out of court after a contentious pretrial contest. The judge said that Falwell, and other people who "invite attention and publicity by their own voluntary actions," couldn't limit First Amendment freedoms simply because they didn't like a particular publication. In a press conference on national television, the caustic attorney for *Penthouse* deliberately mispronounced Falwell's name, calling him "Foulwell." The attorney: Norman Roy Grutman. Morality for Falwell was a highly flexible concept; forgiveness was, too. He wasn't prepared to forgive me for my ad parody, but he was quite willing to forgive Grutman for mocking him on national television and unmercifully gutting his lawsuit against *Penthouse*. When he wanted to win a tough court case, a shark is what he sought. In Bob Guccione's attorney, he found one.

When I moved to Los Angeles, I had begun doing business with an L.A. law firm and its senior partner, Alan Isaacman. I chose Alan to head the defense team in the Falwell suit. Alan had credentials equal to Grutman's, but a completely different style and personality. Like Grutman he had received an Eastern education, having attended Pennsylvania State University and Harvard Law School. Alan had then worked as a federal public defender and in a number of private firms on the West Coast before starting his own practice in Beverly Hills. He had a reputation as an excellent trial lawyer in both civil and criminal cases. But Alan was easygoing, informal, and unpretentious. His boyish looks and disarming openness made people like him and feel comfortable. He was good for me because he did not fit anyone's stereotype of a pornographer's lawyer. There was no suggestion of sleaze about him. Alan didn't even subscribe to *Hustler*.

Falwell had Grutman file a complaint on his home turf, the United States District Court for the Western District of Virginia. The case was assigned to Judge James Turk in Roanoke, the very same judge who had thrown out Falwell's suit against *Penthouse* when Grutman had represented Guccione. Falwell's suit sought damages on three different legal grounds. The first claim in the complaint was that *Hustler* and I had appropriated Falwell's name and likeness for the purposes of "advertisement or trade" without his consent. The second claim was for libel. Falwell alleged that I had made false and defamatory statements; that is, I had committed "illegal, immoral, and reprehensible acts, [implying] that [Falwell was] an alcoholic and that he [was] insincere and hypocritical in his work as a fundamentalist minister." The third claim was that I had intentionally inflicted emotional distress (translation: I had hurt his feelings). The third count said that in publishing the Campari ad, *Hustler* and I had "acted willfully, intentionally, recklessly, and maliciously [with conduct that was] outrageous, extreme, and intolerable in that it offend[ed] generally accepted standards of decency and morality." Grutman, who had written the complaint, presumably knew a great deal about decency and morality from his work with Guccione.

One of the first steps Grutman took after filing Falwell's complaint was to schedule a deposition so that he could question me in some detail about my motive in publishing the parody. At the time of the deposition, I was still in federal detention in Butner, North Carolina. But Grutman scheduled the deposition, and pursued it vigorously, even though he knew I was in no shape to be deposed. He arrived at a time when I was sick, drugged, angry, and overcome with pain. Understandably, I wasn't in the mood to cooperate with anyone—particularly someone as obnoxious and imperious as Grutman. In my misery I felt betrayed by everyone except Althea. I wasn't even sure I could trust my own attorneys.

When the day of the deposition arrived, I was wheeled down to a conference room from my cell, handcuffed to a gurney. I was dirty, bearded, and covered with bedsores. I couldn't move my legs, of course, and still had the round-the-clock sensation that they were on fire. I felt like a wounded animal, reduced to the most basic instincts of fear and suspicion. As the orderly pushed me through the door, I could see Alan Isaacman and David Kahn, my own attorneys; Grutman; several prison officials; a court reporter; and a video technician. I knew I was in for a bad experience.

Grutman skipped the niceties, didn't greet me, turned to the camera operator, and said, "Videotape on, please. Are the voice levels satisfactory?" He then turned to the court reporter and said, "Administer the oath to Mr. Flynt." The reporter looked at my shackled hands and said, "Can you raise your right hand?" "No, they're cuffed," I said, stating the obvious. Ignoring my response, the reporter continued, "Do you solemnly swear that the testimony you are about to give is the truth, the whole truth, and nothing but the truth, so help you God?" "No, not until you take the cuffs off," I replied. What did they think I was going to do, leap off the gurney and strangle Grutman? It was a nice thought, but not much of a risk.

Isaacman and Grutman then argued about my shackles. Alan wanted the cuffs removed so that the videotape testimony—which would presumably be shown to a jury—would seem as normal and unprejudicial as possible. Grutman offered to shoot the scene from the shoulders up, and Alan agreed to the compromise. I interrupted and said that I would have to take a break every twenty minutes to do a series of exercises, called "depressions," to keep the blood circulating in my legs. Grutman agreed. But I was still not happy. I had a severe bedsore on my back that had not been attended to, and I wanted it treated before I began; and I still did not want to proceed as long as I was shackled to the gurney. Grutman ignored my concerns and proceeded as though I had said nothing. "Mr. Flynt, the oath has been administered to you. You heard the oath. Do you swear to tell the truth and nothing but the truth, so help you God?" "No," I answered firmly.

Grutman reflected on my negative answer for a brief moment, glanced at the camera, and then said, "Will you tell me, sir, please, whether you will *affirm* to tell the truth, the whole truth, and nothing but the truth?" "No," I said, a little louder, "I will never affirm to tell the truth as long as these handcuffs are on, Mr. Grutman." "I take it you have no *religious* objection to taking the oath; is that correct?" said Grutman, carefully emphasizing the word *religious*. "I'll swear on anything, Mr. Grutman, to get these cuffs off. I'll declare you God, but I'm not talking to you with them on," I replied. Grutman was clearly irritated and proceeded to lecture me about my responsibility to cooperate with the court-ordered deposition. Without breaking stride, he finished his lecture and began asking questions. "Mr. Flynt, what is your full name?" he asked. I still had the cuffs on and wasn't about to cooperate in any way. "Fuck you," I thought to myself. I gave him a bullshit answer. "Christopher Cornwallis I.P.Q. Harvey H. Pagey Pugh. They call me Larry Flynt. . . ."

Over the next several minutes the deposition turned into a circus. I became more and more angry, and as I did, the pain raging through my body rose, too. My legs burned, my head throbbed, and my frustration grew. After a while I lost control. I tried to fire my attorneys, I demanded medical attention, and I lashed out verbally at Grutman. Alan thought I had gone off the deep end and desperately tried to end the deposition. As Grutman scrambled to bring order, he shouted, "Listen, Mr. Flynt . . . !" I yelled back, "No, you listen to me, asshole . . . shut up!" A medical attendant had come in. I turned to him and said, "Will you dress my bedsore?" Grutman halted the deposition, asking for a recess. I had won a temporary victory.

During the recess my medical needs were attended to, and half an hour later I was wheeled back into the conference room. Grutman was finally ready to accede to my demand to have the handcuffs removed as a precondition to testifying. As the attendant parked my gurney in front of the court reporter and the video camera, Grutman said, "If I ask the captain to remove your handcuffs, will you give me a real deposition?" "Yes," I answered. Grutman looked at Captain Silvey, who was standing at the back of the room, and said, "Captain, will you remove his handcuffs?" Silvey nodded yes, walked over, and removed my cuffs. I was now willing to talk, but I was feeling somewhat confused and disoriented. Only my anger remained distinct and unchanged. Every question Grutman asked me was a pretext for another angry outburst.

From a legal standpoint the deposition was a disaster for me. The way I was feeling, I couldn't have cared less. When you feel as bad as I did, nothing but instinct is left. Grutman scored one important legal victory after another. Alan Isaacman was beside himself with frustration and concern. Alan repeatedly objected, ordered me not to answer questions, and argued with Grutman. But it was all to no avail. I didn't care what anyone was thinking. I didn't care about strategy. I didn't care what people might think of me.

I was trying to protect the only thing left that seemed real: the integrity of my anger. As far as I was concerned, there was no justice, no God, no rationality left in the world. The government had done nothing to find or arrest the man who had shot me, the medical profession had done little or nothing to alleviate my pain, and the legal profession was persecuting me for expressing my passionately held opinion that Jerry Falwell was a religious phony. My anger flowed out, unmediated by reason and unfettered by any conception of "civilized" discourse. Yet in the midst of my seemingly demented performance, my humanity was somehow preserved. That pompous asshole, Norman Grutman, could not penetrate the center of my psyche. I absorbed every blow he delivered and gave nothing up. I responded with unrepentant candor, crude humor, and pure fantasy. Grutman had finally found a person he could not intimidate, and it frustrated him enormously. He couldn't make me squirm.

In the months preceding the deposition I had managed to raise the ire of Grutman and Falwell above the boiling point. Grutman had been featured in *Hustler* as its "Asshole of the Month," as had Jerry Falwell. In one issue I had published a cartoon showing an old lady in a rat-infested apartment, in shabby clothes, with a dog food can next to her and a single bare lightbulb hanging over her head. She was writing a letter that read, "Dear Jerry Falwell, I want to thank you for the inspiration and comfort your television broadcasts give me. I am enclosing the remainder of my Social Security money to help you keep up your

fine work, as I know you need it." In another issue I
ran a cartoon showing the devil sitting behind a big
executive desk, talking into a speakerphone. The devil
was saying, "Send Falwell in here. I want to see the look
on the fucker's face." It was inconvenient for Grutman—and impossible for Falwell—to admit that I was
engaging in legitimate social commentary. But I was.
They hated me for pointing out their money-
grubbing hypocrisy and the ways in which the Moral
Majority exploited the poor.

As the day of the trial approached, the personal calum-
ny continued. Alan Isaacman decided to file two preliminary motions with Judge Turk. The first was to
throw out the deposition, and the second to throw out
Norman Roy Grutman. Alan's first motion argued that
I was in the manic phase of a manic-depressive cycle
and was too highly medicated to testify rationally.
Included with the motion were two affidavits from
psychiatrists who had determined that I was at the
peak of a manic-depressive episode at the time of the
deposition, and consequently not in my rational
mind. Grutman countered that I had been feigning
incompetence to "justify [my] intentional campaign of
personal vilification." The second motion complained
that Grutman had "indisputably crossed over the line
separating zealous representation from fanatical disregard for the precepts of professional responsibility and
even criminal law." The basis of the claim was a body
of incriminating evidence suggesting that he had paid
a witness to testify against me.

The charges against Grutman were well founded. Falwell had provided money to Grutman (by means of a so-called "legal expense" paid to Grutman's firm) to induce a disgruntled former bodyguard of mine, Bill Rider, to make a sworn statement that I had announced in his presence my intention to "get Falwell." The claim was bogus, but with the considerable motivation of a $10,000 payment (in our opinion, a bribe), Rider had agreed to make the statement and provide a copy of the Campari ad parody with my initials on it approving its content. (In fact, we had already provided a copy of the ad with my initials on it; the request was a cynical attempt by Grutman to avoid the appearance of bribery.) Alan provided the court with copies of letters from Grutman confirming the payment and conditions Rider was to meet prior to collecting his check. And, in addition to the $10,000, another inducement had been offered: Falwell would release Rider from any legal liability arising from the transaction. At the bottom of the letter was the following signature: "Norman Roy Grutman, Attorney for Rev. Jerry Falwell." Falwell was quite willing to bludgeon me with the biblical injunction against "bearing false witness" while at the same time his attorney was out using Falwell's cash to induce a witness to testify against me. As far as we were concerned, the whole arrangement was both illegal and unethical. Federal bribery statutes prohibited the payment of money "to any person, for . . . testimony under oath . . . as a witness." And further, the statutes also provided that anyone who "directly or indirectly, corruptly gives, offers, or promises anything of value to any person . . . with intent to influence the testimony under oath of such person, shall be guilty of a felony."

I had frequently been the victim of a double legal standard and a widespread prejudice among jurists and juries against pornographers. I was not surprised, therefore, when Judge Turk ruled against both motions. He wavered at first, initially banning the use of my deposition, but then caved in to Grutman. On the matter of dismissing Grutman from the case, the judge demonstrated a high degree of ambiguity—he was obviously not pleased with Grutman's tactics but refused to remove him. As one commentator said, "In the end Judge Turk dropped back fifteen yards and punted. He ruled for Grutman, but at the same time he delivered a cryptic jab at 'attorney misconduct. . . .'" In his decision Turk said: "[Disqualification is a] drastic measure which courts should hesitate to impose except when absolutely necessary. . . . Indeed, courts have previously declined to disqualify counsel even though the court had serious misgivings about counsel's conduct, and even though the court found that the attorney had in fact violated the canons of professional ethics . . . therefore, although the court does not condone attorney misconduct, it declines to dismiss the action or to disqualify counsel for the plaintiff." In other words, Grutman was guilty as hell, but Turk didn't have the courage to dismiss him.

By the time the day of the trial arrived, I had already been released from federal detention and was feeling more like my normal self. I flew in and settled into a hotel suite. Falwell arrived on his home turf in his own luxury airplane. Falwell was every bit as much a "hustler" as I was, frequently traveling with a large entourage, wearing expensive suits, and looking like a well-to-do corporate executive—which he was. His tax-exempt ministerial "housing allowance" helped subsidize his luxurious home, and his airplane and car were leased by the nonprofit corporation he headed. The numerous perquisites of his position allowed him to take a relatively small salary—good for public relations and fund-raising—while maintaining a very high standard of living. "At least I pay taxes on what I make," I thought, "and so does my corporation." I wondered how many people were aware of the gap between his "good ol' boy" Baptist image and the reality of his lifestyle.

After the jury was selected and brief opening statements were made, the trial commenced with Grutman examining his star witness, Jerry Falwell. He began by eliciting the fact that Falwell was a local boy, born and bred in Virginia, and then proceeded to work through a carefully constructed agenda. Falwell, with cool understatement, reviewed his perception of what the issues were in the case, tried to defuse the impression that he, too, was a hustler, explained his moral agenda for America, and preached a little, making the point that my behavior was not merely a personal insult but an example of how America's moral agenda had failed. Then Grutman led him through a series of questions related to the Campari ad. "Mr. Falwell, is drinking alcohol something that you avoid or not do?" he asked. Falwell replied, "Since I became a Christian in 1952, I have been and am a teetotaler." "Have you ever sponsored, endorsed, or promoted the advertisement of any alcoholic beverages?" "Never at any time," Falwell said firmly. "Have you ever taken alcoholic beverages before going into the pulpit to deliver your message or address your congregation?" "Never at any time," he said, repeating a litany that would go on endlessly.

After dozens of intervening questions, all intended to place Falwell somewhere near the right hand of God, Grutman zeroed in on the issue of his mother. "You have described your mother in earlier testimony as a woman closest to a saint that you have ever known. To your knowledge, Mr. Falwell, was your mother a morally correct woman insofar as her personal life was concerned?" "Without a blemish," Falwell replied. Grutman paused as a hush fell over the courtroom. This was well-rehearsed theater; the only thing it lacked was lights and music. Grutman continued. "Forgive the question, but I must ask it: Was your mother anyone who ever committed incest?" At this point Alan rose from his chair to disturb the beatific vision Grutman was creating of Falwell's late mother. "Your honor, excuse me, it seems to me that we could certainly stipulate to that. . . ." "Thanks a lot," grumped Grutman, breaking the mood, "but I want the evidence." Judge Turk let Grutman continue. "Mr. Falwell, specifically, did you and your mother ever commit incest?" "Absolutely not," Falwell boomed, looking right at me.

Grutman, who was still *Penthouse*'s lawyer, then proceeded to question Falwell on the contents of *Hustler*, with the express aim of creating a sense of outrage among the jurors. Considering the fact that Grutman's primary career specialty had been the *defense* of pornography, his indignant tone was an act of extreme cynicism, if not outright fraud. He handed Falwell a copy of *Hustler* and began to ask him questions about it. "Does it show naked women lewdly exposing themselves?" he asked. "It does," Falwell replied. "Does it have advertisements for sexual aids and mechanical devices?" "Yes." "When you saw your picture on the inside cover of a magazine that contained such contents, how did you feel about that, Mr. Falwell?" "It would be difficult to describe my emotions because I have never in my life seen such a despicable array of garbage." Grutman then turned Falwell's attention to the inside front page of *Hustler*, where the ad parody appeared. Grutman ignored the fact that the ad was parodic and read every line as if it were a statement of fact, frequently paused, and gave Falwell the opportunity to state the obvious: that he had never been drunk, had sex with his mother, etcetera. Grutman finished his examination of Falwell with the following question: "With respect to the materials that I have shown to you in this case, what is your reaction or response to it in terms of your feelings?" Falwell replied, "It is the most hurtful, damaging, despicable, low-type personal attack that I can imagine one human being can inflict upon another."

Later in the trial Grutman continued the theme of Falwell as "moral exemplar" by calling on Senator

Jesse Helms as a character witness. Helms said, "In my judgment, there is no finer citizen than Jerry Falwell. He is easily one of the most dedicated men, not only to his noble profession, but to this country. Words escape me to describe what this man means to so many, including me." Words, however, had seldom escaped Jesse in the past. A few years earlier he had reputedly called the University of North Carolina (UNC) the "University of Niggers and Communists." Falwell preferred the company of racists over pornographers—a dubious moral choice.

Grutman had tried to put the whole pornographic enterprise on trial and deflect attention away from the chief legal issues. As I talked to reporters outside the courtroom after Falwell's testimony, I tried to keep those issues in focus. "This is a libel case, not an obscenity case," I told them. "I know I'm in the minority. I know I'm not everybody's cup of tea. But I have a significant readership." My turn to testify came a day later. Grutman had already questioned Falwell at length and shown an edited version of my videotaped deposition. The jury was expecting, I suppose, the devil incarnate. But I was in a calm, lucid state when I took the oath and Alan started asking me questions. He began by asking me about the videotaped deposition. We had some damage control to do. "I feel fine today," I said, "but at the time of the deposition I was in terrible pain. I'd been in solitary confinement for several months—handcuffed to my bed most of the time." Alan asked questions that provided me an opportunity to explain how the madness of my deposition had done nothing to compromise my belief in the First Amendment or abrogate my right to publish outrageous satires of public figures. I described several ad parodies *Hustler* had run over the years. These included the Marlboro Man in the hay with his horse, smoking a cigarette; and a Coca-Cola ad featuring John DeLorean saying, "Things go better with Coke."

After I had described the other ad parodies *Hustler* had run—and elicited a few laughs—Alan asked me the big question: "What did you intend to convey with the Campari ad?" "Well," I began, "we wanted to poke fun at Campari for their advertisements and the innuendos in them. Their ad copy left the question open: Were people talking about their first sexual experience or the first time they drank Campari? To make the ad funny, we needed to have a person that was the complete opposite of what you would expect. If I had been featured in the ad, the parody would not have worked. But if somebody like Reverend Falwell is in it, it is very obvious that he wouldn't do any of those things; that they are not true; that it's not to be taken seriously." "Did you intend to damage Reverend Falwell's reputation?" he asked next. "If I wanted to hurt Reverend Falwell, we would do a serious article on the inside and make it an investigative exposé and talk about his jet or whether he has a Swiss bank account. If you really want to hurt someone, you print something that is *believable*." "Then the ad was not intended to be taken seriously?" "Falwell making it with his mother?" I replied. "No one can find that believable!"

"What effect, if any, did you intend for the ad parody to have on Jerry Falwell?" "Well," I said, "we were responding to our own readership; we didn't intend for it to have any effect on him. And the fact that he has responded with this lawsuit is as unbelievable as the ad is."

As he came to the end of his examination, Alan asked me a few questions to clarify my motives in regard to the cartoons I had run about Falwell. In particular, he wanted me to comment on the one about the poor wretch sending her last Social Security dollars to support his ministry. "It wasn't necessarily in good taste," I said, "but you must realize that there are a great number of people who should not be solicited for money. This is a contention raised in letters to *Hustler*, not only about Reverend Falwell, but in regard to other evangelists, too. *Hustler* satirizes and parodies issues of sex, politics, and religion—that is our entire editorial focus." "What about your column 'Asshole of the Month'?" Alan asked. "It's an award that we give every month to various people," I said. "We try to feature people who appear to be hypocritical or inconsistent in their philosophy. I've named myself 'Asshole of the Month,' along with everyone from the President of the United States to Pat Boone."

When Alan Isaacman sat down, Norman Roy Grutman stood up, paused for dramatic effect, and asked, in his usual stentorian tone: "I notice in your examination today that in answering the questions put to you by your counsel, there was not a single obscenity, not a single vile word uttered by you. Is the Larry Flynt that we are seeing here in court today the real Larry Flynt, or is the real Larry Flynt the one we saw on the television screen in your June 15 deposition?" He was baiting the hook for me, but I wasn't biting. "I'm under treatment," I said calmly. "I'm more myself today. I didn't use any obscenities because I saw no need to offend this jury." Grutman turned, picked up a *Hustler* from the plaintiff's table, walked back over to me, and said, "I'll stand alongside of you, and you can read with me." He was holding the June 1976 issue of *Hustler*. He read aloud: "[*Hustler*] will [always] report matters as we see them, in the same forthright, down-to-earth manner. Whether a person is a private citizen or a public figure, if he's an asshole, a shithead, or a scumbag, that's just the way you'll see him in *Hustler*." He paused again. "What's your question?" I asked. "If you think someone is an asshole, a shithead, or a scumbag, you're going to say so in your magazine—right? Just answer *yes* or *no*."

I refused to fall into Grutman's trap. "I think everyone is an asshole because everyone's got one," I said. "And if something cannot be defined, it's not libelous. You are talking about an editorial opinion. It may be in bad taste, but am I being persecuted because of my taste, or am I being sued for libel?" Grutman ignored my answer. "Mr. Flynt, have you ever said, 'Free expression is absolute'?" "Yes," I replied, "as long as no one is hurt." "And *absolute* means you can say whatever you want?" "Yes," I said, "I feel you have a right to say whatever you want to."

"No matter how somebody's feelings may be affected?"
"Ah!" I said. "You are talking about matters of taste.
What I'm trying to say is that no one should be
imprisoned for what they say! If you don't like what is
being said on television, turn it off. If you don't like
what's in *Hustler*, don't buy it." Grutman and I continued to spar for over two hours. Over Alan's objections, Grutman introduced several articles and quotes
from *Hustler*, none relevant to the case, and all meant
to prejudice the jury and convince them that I was the
foulest, grossest man on the planet. It was partially
true. I often was foul and gross. But what did that have
to do with the issues we were litigating? Nothing. It
was an *ad hominem* legal strategy that did little to illu-
minate the important First Amendment issues that
were at stake.

With my testimony over, the evidence was in, and both
sides presented their closing arguments. Alan Isaacman reiterated our position: The Campari ad was a
joke, a parody, and was never intended to be taken seriously. "It would be ridiculous," he argued, "to base an
award of damages on the basis of something as frivo-
lous as hurt feelings." Grutman's closing statement
was intended to create a sense of horror within the
jurors. I was a crass and foul man, he preached to the
jury, and it was their responsibility to draw the line
against my outrageous behavior. He was beginning to
sound like Simon Leis. "Certainly the eyes of the country are on Roanoke," he said. "And you are going to
make a statement. And that statement that you are

going to make from this courthouse is going to spread throughout the length and breadth of this land. The nation is watching. The nation wants to know where the Constitution stands. Are you going to let loose chaos and anarchy? Are you going to turn America into the Planet of the Apes?"

When Grutman had finished his performance, Judge Turk gave the jury his final instructions, carefully explaining the rules of law that applied to the case. He barred the jury from considering the claim that the Campari ad had constituted an appropriation of Falwell's name and likeness "for purposes of trade" without his permission. We were not trying to sell Campari, he ruled, and therefore the charge was baseless. The two issues before them, he explained, were the matters of libel and the intentional infliction of emotional distress. The merit of the libel charge, he said, depended on the question of whether the ad could "reasonably be understood as describing actual facts about plaintiff or actual events in which plaintiff participated." If the jury decided that the answer to that question was "yes," then they had to consider a second one: Did I publish the ad with "actual malice"? The definition of "actual malice," he explained, was "knowledge of falsity, or reckless disregard for the truth." Turk then explained the charge of "intentional infliction of emotional distress." They must decide, he said, whether I had acted intentionally to inflict emotional distress on Reverend Falwell; and further, if I had, whether the ad offended generally accepted standards of decency.

The jury did not deliberate long. Alan called me the next day to say that the verdict was in, and that he would meet me at the courthouse. My assistant wheeled me in through the wooden gate and into position behind the defendant's table. Judge Turk entered, and a few moments later, the jury. The clerk read the verdict. As to the count of libel: *for the defendant*. No reasonable person could have understood the ad as factual. As to the infliction of emotional distress: *for the plaintiff*. Did the ad offend generally accepted standards of decency? Yes. Falwell had won a partial victory. The jury awarded him $100,000 in compensatory damages and $100,000 in punitive damages. In spite of the fine I was elated. I had been very worried about the outcome. I was afraid that the jury would put me out of business. The fine was a slap on the wrist compared to what could have happened. I weighed my options. It would cost me more to pursue the case on appeal than it would to pay the fine. I might lose. The stakes, however, were very high. A constitutional principle was at stake. We immediately filed an appeal with the United States Court of Appeals, Fourth Circuit.

On August 5, 1986, a three-judge panel of the appeals court rendered its decision. It was a bombshell. The panel refused to overturn the Falwell decision. For the first time in a major case, the court upheld the concept that liability could be predicated on mere intent to inflict emotional distress, even though the published material was neither libelous nor an invasion of privacy. In rendering its decision, the court considered a supremely important precedent-setting case: *New York Times Co. v. Sullivan** (the basis on which Judge Turk made his instructions to the jury). The press considered the *Sullivan* decision holy writ, and every publisher in the country was suddenly nervous. Had the court abandoned the *Sullivan* decision? We wanted another hearing—this time with the entire panel of Fourth Circuit judges (a type of hearing referred to as *en banc*). Alan filed a request for an *en banc* hearing. One Fourth Circuit Judge, J. Harvie Wilkinson III, after having reviewed our request, wrote an eloquent appeal to his fellow jurists, arguing that an *en banc* rehearing should be granted. Wilkinson was arguably the finest scholar on the Fourth Circuit, a graduate of Yale and the University of Virginia Law School. He had been a law professor at Virginia and was the author of several books. Wilkinson did his best, but the circuit voted six to five against a rehearing. We filed a petition with the United States Supreme Court— our last hope.

---

* *New York Times Co. v. Sullivan* is a landmark 1964 Supreme Court decision in which the court overturned a libel conviction for a paid advertisement in the *Times* attacking Southern racism and police brutality. An Alabama jury had awarded a Montgomery police commissioner, L. B. Sullivan, $500,000 for alleged libels contained in the ad. The court ruled that citizens had the right to speak against the government and its officials without fear of prosecution for "seditious libel"—slander against the state.

The United States Supreme Court receives thousands of petitions a year, and it is the rare case that gets accepted for review. In an average year about 150 cases get a full hearing. Only the most pressing and important ones are ever considered. Most cases that come before the court are the result of petitions for *certiorari*. Lawyers are fond of Latin terms. *Certiorari* is from a word that means "to be informed." If the court grants a petition, it agrees to review the facts of a particular case—to "inform itself." Alan filed a petition for *certiorari* with the court, asking it to exercise its discretion and review our case; and Grutman, of course, filed a response asking it to deny the review and leave the Fourth Circuit's decision alone. When a petition is filed with the court, outside parties, unrelated to the plaintiffs, are allowed to file advisory briefs known as *amicus curiae*, or "friend of the court" briefs. When Falwell had originally sued, no one was willing to stand up with me and file an *amicus curiae* brief, either at the original trial or the appeal. No surprise there. The mainstream press lacked moral courage and was afraid that the justices would only affirm the lower court's decision, establishing a new precedent. And they all thought I was too unseemly to associate with. However, solely on the basis of my own initiative—and with no support from any outside organization—my attorneys prevailed, and on March 20, 1987, the Supreme Court granted my petition for a writ of *certiorari* to review the Fourth Circuit's decision.

Suddenly I had a lot friends—reluctant ones. Now that the stakes were so high and the issues so clear, the mainstream media began to change their minds. If the Fourth Circuit's opinion was left standing, First Amendment rights—rights that had evolved through court decisions for over thirty years to protect freedom of speech and the press—would quickly unravel. The first media organization brave enough to cast its lot with me was the *Richmond Times-Dispatch* and its sister publication, the *Richmond News Leader*. But others followed, and soon the trickle of *amicus curiae* briefs turned into a flood. Weighing in on my side were the New York Times Company, the (Los Angeles) Times Mirror Company, the Virginia Press Association, the American Newspaper Association, the Magazine Publishers Association, HBO, the ACLU, the Authors League of America, the Association of American Editorial Cartoonists, and political satirist Mark Russell. It was a who's who of the American publishing industry.

The court set the date for oral arguments for the morning of December 2, 1987. Only eight justices would hear my case. Justice Lewis Powell had resigned from the court in the spring, and an intense battle over his successor had ensued. President Reagan had nominated Robert Bork, but after a contentious hearing the Senate had refused to confirm him. Reagan's second choice was Douglas Ginsburg, but Ginsburg's nomination went down in flames when it was revealed that he had smoked a joint while a professor at Harvard. Reagan's third choice, Anthony Kennedy, had been confirmed, but had not yet assumed the bench. Several of the remaining justices were old farts in their seventies or eighties. The chief justice was William Rehnquist, who had replaced Earl Warren in September 1986. Rehnquist was a Nixon appointee. He had almost always voted against the press in First Amendment cases—and had done so more than twenty times. Rehnquist's only redeeming quality, we thought, was that he had a reputation for possessing a good sense of humor. We didn't know how he or any other justice would vote, but we had every reason to expect the outcome was in doubt. According to a survey of Supreme Court pundits Alan had made, Rehnquist and at least five other justices were predisposed toward Falwell.

The hearing took place on a cold, wintry day. Alan Isaacman arrived at the court building before I did, as did Grutman, and entered through a door reserved for attorneys. I entered the courtroom after all the attorneys had arrived, through a side door, and sat about twenty feet from Falwell, on the same side of the room. The courtroom was packed. Pulitzer Prize-winning *New York Times* reporter Anthony Lewis was there with several third-year students he had brought from a law and Constitution class he was teaching at Harvard Law School. Alan's mother had come to see her son's moment of glory; so had Grutman's wife. In a special section reserved for attorneys who had been admitted to the Supreme Court Bar, two lawyers sat: Roslyn Mazer and Harriette Dorsen. Mazer had written the *amicus curiae* brief for the cartoonists' association; and

Dorsen was vice-president and general counsel for Doubleday, and an expert on satire and parody.

Supreme Court hearings are relatively short, with each side allotted only thirty minutes to make their arguments. A warning light on the podium signals the attorneys when their time is up. Generally, an argument is not a speech but a dialogue with the justices, who frequently interrupt and ask questions. It is a give-and-take process, and the measure of a good attorney is not necessarily oratorical skill, but the ability to think on his feet. Alan and Grutman were sitting at their respective counsel tables, reviewing their notes and doing their best to anticipate the kind of questions that might be asked of them. The spectators were speaking in low tones, as if they were in church. Suddenly the eight justices filed out from behind a red velvet curtain and stood behind their high-backed judge's chairs, looking out over the bench. In a loud voice a marshal called out, "All rise!" As everyone stood, he pronounced the traditional greeting: "Oyez, oyez, oyez. The honorable, the chief justice and the associate justices of the Supreme Court of the United States. All persons having business before this honorable court are admonished to draw nigh and give their attention, for the court is now sitting. God save the United States and this honorable court."

When the justices had sat down, Chief Justice Rehnquist looked at his notes and said, "We'll hear the argument first this morning in number 86-1278, *Hustler Magazine and Larry C. Flynt* versus *Jerry Falwell*." He then nodded at Alan, who was already

standing at the podium. "Mr. Isaacman, you may proceed whenever you are ready." Alan, looking relaxed in
spite of the august occasion, addressed the court:

> Mr. Chief Justice, and may it please the court.
> The First Amendment protects all speech
> except for certain narrowly drawn categories.
> For example, the First Amendment does not
> protect false statements of fact made with req-
> uisite fault. The First Amendment doesn't
> protect obscene speech . . . [or] fighting words
> made in the presence of the person to whom
> the words are addressed and likely to incite
> violence. This case raises as a general ques-
> tion whether the Court should expand the
> areas left unprotected by the First Amend-
> ment and create another exception to pro-
> tected speech. And in this situation, the new
> area that is sought to be protected is satiric or
> critical commentary of a public figure which
> does not contain any assertions of fact.

After his opening statement, Alan continued to
build his case, fielding questions from the justices and
trying to steer the discussion in the direction he wanted it to go. He was interrupted several times, asked
to clarify some points, challenged on some of his
assumptions; yet for the most part he avoided any serious pitfalls. About two-thirds of the way through his
presentation, Justice Stevens asked him, "What is the

public interest that you're describing . . . that there's some interest in making [Falwell] look ludicrous? What is the public interest?" Stevens had given Alan the perfect opportunity to drive a point home. Smiling at Stevens, he said:

> There is a public interest in having *Hustler* express its view that what Jerry Falwell says . . . is B.S. And *Hustler* has every right to say that somebody who's out there campaigning against it, saying . . . we're poison on the minds of America . . . is full of B.S. And that is what this ad parody says. [The ad parody] puts him in a ridiculous setting. Instead of Jerry Falwell speaking from the television with a beatific look on his face . . . and a Bible in his hand, . . . *Hustler* is saying, 'Let's deflate this stuffed shirt; let's bring him down to our level. . . .'

At this point the whole courtroom broke out in laughter, including all the justices. Chief Justice Rehnquist laughed so hard he almost fell out of his seat. I was told later that no one could remember another instance when the court broke out in laughter. Ordinarily it was a quiet and staid place. Alan had broken the tension and scored a major point. "Perhaps Rehnquist's sense of humor is working in my favor," I thought.

Justice Scalia then changed the line of questioning. "Mr. Isaacman," he said, "the First Amendment is not everything. It's a very important value, but it's not the only value in our society. You're giving us no help in trying to balance it. . . . The rule you give us says that if you stand for public office, or become a public figure, you cannot protect yourself against a parody of committing incest with your mother in an outhouse. Do you think George Washington would have stood for public office if that was the consequence?" "Well," Alan responded, "there is a cartoon in the brief of the Association of American Editorial Cartoonists that has George Washington being led on a donkey, and the caption reads something to the effect that the man leading the donkey is also leading an ass." "I can handle that," Justice Scalia said, "and I think George could handle that, too." Again the courtroom burst into laughter. Alan was on a roll.

The questions continued for a few more minutes, until the warning light went on. Noticing it, Alan said:

> And in summing up, what I would like to do is say this is not just a dispute between *Hustler* and Jerry Falwell. It [is a dispute] that affects everything that goes on in our national life. We have a long tradition of satiric commentary, and you can't pick up a newspaper without seeing cartoons or editorials that have critical comments about people. And if Jerry Falwell can sue because he suffered emotional distress, anybody else who is in public would be able to sue because they suffered emotional distress.

Alan looked up to the chief justice as he finished, sig-
naling that he was done. "Thank you, Mr. Isaacman,"
Rehnquist said. Alan turned around, winked at me,
and sat down at the counsel table. He had delivered a
first-class performance—and had obviously enjoyed it.

As Alan Isaacman sat down, Norman Roy Grutman
slowly rose and walked to the podium with the dignified, confident step of someone who considered
himself a demigod. In a sonorous voice he made his
opening statement:

> Mr. Chief Justice, may it please the court.
> Deliberate, malicious character assassina-
> tion is not protected by the First Amend-
> ment to the Constitution. Deliberate, mali-
> cious character assassination is what was
> proven in this case. By the defendant's own
> explicit admission, the publication before
> this court was the product of a deliberate
> plan to assassinate, to upset the character
> and integrity of the plaintiff, and to cause
> him severe emotional disturbance with total
> indifference then and now to the severity of
> the injury caused. When the publication was
> protested by the bringing of this lawsuit, the
> unregenerate defendant published it again.

Grutman exuded a kind of supreme confidence in
his abilities (most people would call it arrogance), and
as he continued to speak and answer questions, his

speech was peppered with stodgy formulations like "I dare say" and hyperbolic adjectives like "heinous" and "loathsome." The justices seemed irritated at what I took to be the world's second biggest stuffed shirt pontificating in front of them. Within a few minutes they were all over him, interrupting and challenging every assertion he was making. They were giving him no quarter. The great man seemed to get a little flustered, and the more flustered he became, the more convoluted his reasoning became. At one point he tried to argue that the Campari ad was intended to be a statement of fact about Falwell (and consequently subject to an important legal precedent), but his reasoning was so obtuse and self-contradictory that Justice Scalia—presumably his ally—just looked at him, dumbfounded. Grutman was trying to argue that even though the Campari ad was not a statement of fact, and though no one believed it was a statement of fact—and in spite of a disclaimer in the ad stating that it was a parody—that it was, *nevertheless*, a statement of fact. It was an "untrue" statement of fact. You could almost hear the justices say a collective "Huh?" Justice Scalia interrupted. "Give me a statement of fact that isn't a statement of fact. When you say 'statement of fact,' it means *true* fact, or means nothing at all."

Grutman, responding to Scalia, sputtered, "No. That is the Aristotelian interpretation of a statement of fact as propounded by Professors Wechsler and Michael in their famous monograph, but in the common parlance in which we speak, a statement of fact is an utterance about either an event, or a thing, or a person which can be proven either true or false. If it's true, then it's a true fact, but if it's false, like gravity causes things to float upward—that's a statement of fact, but it's manifestly false." Grutman had lost it. Not only was he clueless about Aristotelian philosophy, but his former law professor, Herbert Wechsler, had never written any famous monograph on the subject. His argument was pure bullshit. Grutman began to backpedal, but it was too late. The justices pursued him like hounds after a rabbit. After a few more minutes the warning light went on. Grutman glanced down, noted his time had run out, and closed with these words: "This case is no threat to the media. It will be the rare case indeed where this kind of behavior will ever be replicated, but where it occurs, it deserves the condemnation which the jury gave it, which the Fourth Circuit found, and which I respectfully submit this court should affirm. Thank you." Rehnquist thanked him in return, and the oral arguments were complete. There was nothing to do now but wait.

More than a year later, on February 24, 1988, the Supreme Court published its decision. Alan called me at my office. "Larry," he said, "I've got some incredible news." "Incredible?" I thought. "Incredibly bad or incredibly good?" Before I could ask my question, he said, "We won! It was a unanimous decision, 8-0." I took a deep breath and let out a sigh of relief. "The chief justice wrote the decision himself," Alan continued. "I'm sending over a copy." When I received the booklet containing the court's decision, I could see that six justices had joined Rehnquist in the opinion: Justices Brennan, Marshall, Blackmun, Stevens, O'Connor, and Scalia. Justice White had written his own two-sentence concurring opinion.

In the opinion, Rehnquist had quoted a previous landmark case, *FCC* v. *Pacifica Foundation*. Three sentences from that decision stood out in bold relief: "The fact that society may find speech offensive is not a sufficient reason for suppressing it. Indeed, if it is the speaker's opinion that gives offense, that consequence is a reason for according it constitutional protection. For it is a central tenet of the First Amendment that the government must remain neutral in the marketplace of ideas."

It was, by any measure, a stunning decision. All the justices we had expected to vote against us had voted for us! Five years earlier I had called Sandra Day O'Connor a "token cunt" and the rest of the justices (a slightly different cast of characters) "assholes." In spite of my outburst, they had done the right thing. Rodney Smolla, a professor of constitutional law at the College of William and Mary, and an observer at the trial, summed up the meaning of the victory:

> The Supreme Court's opinion in *Falwell* v. *Flynt* is a triumphant celebration of freedom of speech. Far from signaling the disintegration of America's moral gyroscope, the opinion reaffirms the most powerful magnetic force in our constitutional compass: that essential optimism of the American spirit,

an optimism unafraid of wild-eyed pluralistic, free-wheeling debate. We are a good and generous people, but we are not particularly gentle or genteel; we prefer to speak our minds. . . . Thomas Jefferson taught a little rebellion now and then is a good thing. Rebellion is often raucous and disturbing, indecorous and indecent.

Indecorous and indecent? I don't deny it. But the victor, at long last.

10.
Too Numb
to Weep

In 1983—FIVE YEARS AFTER I WAS SHOT, THE SAME month the Campari ad ran in *Hustler*, and after what seemed like an eternity of unrelenting pain—I looked at Althea one afternoon and said, "You look like hell. You gotta take care of yourself. Why don't you go see a doctor?" By that time our lives had been reduced to a daily routine of addiction. I hoped that a doctor might be able to give her some help. I was miserable, but not too miserable to know that I loved that woman. "You're never going to feel right until you stop the drugs," I told her. "I know," she said. "Maybe I will. I've been feeling pretty bad." She had practically stopped eating and was wraith-thin. A doctor put her through a battery of tests, gave her a stern lecture about the necessity of self-care, and sent her home. He said he would call her if anything unusual showed up in the test results.

A few days later Althea took a call on the telephone in our bedroom. It was the doctor. As she listened intently, her gaunt face registered shock, then sadness; and then her expression went blank. She hung up without saying good-bye. Even in my drug-induced stupor I could tell something was wrong. She walked over to the bed, sat down on the edge, and said, "I've got some bad news." "What?" I mumbled. "I've got some real bad news." "What?" I said again. "I have AIDS." The words pierced my consciousness just as those bullets in Lawrenceville had pierced my side. I didn't know what to say, so I just lay there, brushing aside my tears. After a moment I said, "We'll fight this thing." "Why bother?" she said. "It's a death sentence." "I'll send you to the Mayo Clinic; we'll modify your diet and maybe try this holistic medicine thing— maybe it'll improve your immune system. . . ." I rattled off a list of ideas as Althea got up and left the room, searching for her next fix. There was no longer any motivation to break her addiction. She had no interest in helping herself.

For a long time I had harbored the fear that Althea would share a needle with someone and catch hepatitis or AIDS. She had always denied the possibility. "I don't share needles," she said. "I may be a junkie, but I'm a rich junkie. I can afford my own needles." When we learned that she was infected, Althea immediately suspected that she had become HIV-positive as the result of a blood transfusion. She had undergone surgery—a hysterectomy—at Century City Hospital years before. The AIDS virus was just beginning to spread at the time, and blood supplies were not being screened yet. If she hadn't slept with another man—

and I was sure of that, since she preferred women—and if her claim was true about not sharing needles, then her hypothesis was probably correct.

Althea already had a serious drug habit when she was diagnosed with AIDS, but it became much worse afterward. She gave up on life, believing there was no longer any reason to moderate her destructive habits. Her disease was the pretext for an ever more excessive use of cocaine and heroin, and an increasingly out-of-control lifestyle. As the months went by, I found her time and again passed out on the bathroom floor with a needle dangling from her arm. And when she wasn't out cold, she was high. She became a habitué of the Hollywood drug-party scene, a fixture at rock concerts and backstage dope fests, and a regular at the most notorious Sunset Strip clubs. Unaltered, unmediated consciousness was too painful for her to bear, and she never spent a moment without the mind-numbing, soul-searing influence of heroin in her veins. And all the while, I could do nothing but watch: helpless, paralyzed, and in agony.

The next few years were an eternity of pain, but only a brief moment in my life with Althea. My detention in federal prison, my numerous court appearances, my presidential campaign—all these events and more—engaged my time and sapped my limited energy. Althea, preoccupied and distant, had her own life and circle of friends: a dysfunctional entourage of addicts and druggies. We shared a home and saw each other daily, but in a profound sense neither of us was truly present. The stultifying effect of her addiction and of my pain medications altered our relationship and created an unbridgeable gap between us. Our love for each other was undiminished, but our ability to express it was hopelessly impaired. I could do nothing to help her; she, in turn, wanted no help. We lived a day-to-day existence. Our sense of time was compressed. An hour was an eternity. The clock only measured the intervals between her fixes and my doses. Intimacy was impossible; a genuine conversation was difficult; facing reality was out of the question.

On June 27, 1987—after years of living this sad, desperate routine—I was sitting in bed one afternoon, watching television, trying to cope. Althea, stretched out beside me, had been alternately napping and catching squinty-eyed glimpses of the daytime quiz show on the tube. We looked like two zombies with sunken eyes, pallid complexions, and blank expressions. The room was dark. The banal chatter of the quiz-show host and the squeals of anxious contestants filled the room. We didn't talk much; hadn't talked much. Our conversations—if they could be called such—were composed of truncated sentences. As she rose from the bed, I said, "Where . . . ?" "Bath," she mumbled in reply. She shuffled into the bathroom. In a moment I could hear the water running. I turned my attention back to the television. Two or three commercials later I noticed the water was still running. How long had it been? How long had I been watching this stupid show? It was a big bathtub, but it seemed as though it should have been full by now.

Suddenly I was feeling alarmed. My sense of confusion frustrated me. Had the water been running for five minutes or fifteen? I didn't know. The door to the bedroom opened. It was the day nurse. I looked up at her with some relief and said, "Will you check on Althea?" "Of course, Mr. Flynt," she said. Without hesitation she went to the bathroom door, opened it, and went in. The nurse was a small woman, with a big voice. Her scream echoed off the bathroom walls as she bolted back through the door and into the bedroom. Suddenly alert, I shouted, "What's the matter?" "It's Althea!" she yelled. "She's either drowned or drowning!" "Well, for Christ's sake get her out!" I screamed. "You gotta give her artificial respiration!" I felt completely helpless. My wheelchair wasn't next to my bed—there wasn't one damn thing I could do. With some considerable effort the nurse pulled Althea's limp, pale body out of the tub, and into the bedroom, and began administering cardiopulmonary resuscitation. "She's not breathing: She's dead!" the nurse cried. "Don't stop!" I replied, as I reached for the phone and dialed 911.

The paramedics arrived in a few minutes as the nurse continued to administer CPR. They ran up the stairs and into the bedroom, carrying an oxygen bottle, a portable heart monitor, and a tackle box full of medical supplies. Kneeling on the floor, with stethoscopes dangling from their necks and rubber gloves on their hands, they ministered to Althea's lifeless form. But it was no use. She was dead. I sat, still trapped in my bed, and looked across the room at the emaciated, lifeless body that was once Althea. It was too much to take in. I felt numb. I could not weep. I reached for the phone and called Jimmy. He was in Kentucky. "Althea's dead," I told him in a monotone. "I'm sorry, Larry," Jimmy said. "Will you make the funeral arrangements?" I asked. "Yeah," he said, "I'll do that. I'll make the arrangements back here, and you make them there." "Okay," I said. "I'll call you," he replied, and hung up. A few minutes later Althea's doctor arrived to sign the death certificate, and the mortuary attendants came to take her body away. She had taken an overdose of heroin, passed out, and drowned. It was better, I guess, than a lingering death from AIDS.

The numbness continued for the next few days. It was amazing how I could love someone so much yet feel nothing. I had lost the most important person in my life. Althea Leasure Flynt was a unique, irreplaceable, one-of-a-kind person. Why couldn't I feel anything? Perhaps my physical pain blunted my emotional pain; perhaps the consciousness-searing drugs robbed me of the ability to grieve. I didn't know. I didn't complain to God. I didn't believe in God anymore. I just went on, resigned to the circumstances of my fate, unwilling to ask the unanswerable questions.

In the meantime Jimmy had made the funeral arrangements. I wanted to bury Althea in the Flynt family graveyard in Lakeville. So I had the mortuary send her body to Kentucky, and a few days later I followed, flying into the Prestonburg Airport in my jet. Jimmy met me on the tarmac and rode with me into town. We didn't say much. Jimmy had arranged for Bob Harrington to fly in from New Orleans to conduct the funeral. As we rode through the green countryside, I thought about the difference between Althea's public stance on religion and her private beliefs. To those who did not know her, Althea was either indifferent to religion or hostile to it. She had good reason to be hostile. Her experiences with the religious caretakers who had sexually abused her were reason enough. But I knew that in her heart she believed in God. I wanted to honor her belief.

As the car wound its way into the hollow, my mind was filled with the memories of my childhood. My grandparents and great-grandparents were buried there, and so was my little sister, Judy. Now I had come to bury Althea. We passed my father's house, and a newer home Jimmy had built on my father's land. Behind Jimmy's house the hollow sloped up, and on a knoll overlooking the valley—where generations of Flynts had lived—was the family plot. A few simple tombstones marked the spot. The driver parked the car next to Jimmy's house. I could see two or three hundred people gathered around the freshly dug grave and Althea's flower-decked coffin. The mourners stood on the grassy hillside, speaking quietly. On the knoll stood Bob Harrington. I assumed my place at the graveside, sitting in my chair, feeling heavy and lifeless. Harrington delivered a traditional fire-and-brimstone, Southern-style eulogy. I don't remember much of it. My thoughts had turned inward. How could I go on? What was there to live for? I owned one of the most lucrative publishing empires in America. I was wealthy. The U.S. Supreme Court would soon hear my appeal—one of the most important First Amendment cases in the country's history. I had come farther from that Kentucky hillside than I could have imagined in my wildest boyhood dreams. Yet without Althea my life as I knew it seemed over.

Epilogue

Two months after Althea's death I went back to Duke University Hospital for a second operation. The laser-assisted surgery that I had undergone earlier had helped eliminate some of my pain, and the physicians thought they could improve on the first surgery. The procedure, known by its acronym DREZ (which stands for "dorsal root entry zone"), had been steadily refined over the years, and I thought it was worth a try. I spent two weeks in the hospital and returned home feeling much better. Whereas the first operation had relieved my pain level by about one half, the second procedure relieved it by about two-thirds. I still hurt, but the pain was more manageable, and I was significantly improved.

The additional pain relief gave me the energy to concentrate better and work more. I was also able to reduce my pain medications significantly, and the fog that had hung over my consciousness for so many years began to clear. Then in March 1994 I went back for a final DREZ procedure. After this last operation my pain was completely relieved, and I stopped taking any pain medicine at all. When the pain was gone, I no longer had any desire to take drugs. I just stopped overnight, without any complications.

Contrary to published speculations, I did not lose bowel and bladder control after the operations. The whole purpose of the precise, careful DREZ procedure is to avoid a wholesale cauterization of nerves. The surgery is conducted under a microscope and is highly accurate. It took multiple surgeries to relieve the pain because of the conservative approach of the surgeons, who did not want to sever anything but the sensory nerves responsible for my pain. Neither did the procedure leave me impotent. I still have sensation in my genitals, and with the aid of a penile implant I have been able to resume a sex life. There are limitations on my sexual abilities, of course, but it is still a source of genuine pleasure for me.

I have left my religious conversion behind and settled into a comfortable state of atheism. I have come to think that religion has caused more harm than any other idea since the beginning of time. The Jerry Falwells of this world are living proof of the hypocrisy and greed that permeates organized religion in America and around the world. I have worked hard to understand the roots of my own religious conversion. I think my conversion—which was probably typical in many ways—was the outcome of a manic-depressive episode. Perhaps it was the result of a chemical imbalance in my brain. I have had excellent psychiatric resources available to me over the past few years, and have been able to control my own propensity for manic depression. Most people do not have similar resources and turn to family, friends, or local pastors when they experience visions, voices, or other religious phenomena. I believe many of them could be helped by lithium or psychotropic drugs. I have made peace with myself and no longer need religion to find meaning for my life. I have become brutally realistic. I think life is like an assembly line—you get on and at some point you drop off. There is no meaning beyond the present.

No one was arrested for shooting me. Through the years of my pain and paranoia, I proffered many theories. Neither the small-town Lawrenceville police, the FBI, nor any other law-enforcement agency seemed willing or able to identify, much less apprehend, a suspect. Nevertheless, I was never particularly interested in who shot me—the question that haunted me was: *Why*? Why would someone want to assassinate me simply because he disagreed with my views, or my right to publish *Hustler*? Finally a white supremacist, Joseph Paul Franklin—who is currently serving two consecutive life sentences for racially motivated murders—confessed to shooting me. Like so many other right-wing extremists, Franklin was appalled by pornography and offended by an interracial photo spread featured in an early issue of *Hustler*.

As my physical pain began to recede, I resumed my former active role in managing *Hustler* and my other business interests. I found it easier to deal with Althea's loss if I was busy and involved. The many years of pain, drugs, prosecutions, and losses—both physical and emotional—were converted into creative energy. Since 1987 I have started fifteen successful new magazines (on a variety of special interests including electronics, computers, music, and sports), and strengthened my company's position in the marketplace. *Hustler* is now licensed in ten new foreign markets. There are now a total of fifteen foreign editions of *Hustler*. In addition to the print versions, I have also established an electronic edition on the Internet. The *Hustler Online* Website is currently receiving about eight hundred thousand "hits" daily (of which several thousand log on). And recently I started a new sex and pop culture magazine for the Generation-X market entitled *Rage*. To house all of these ventures I bought a new, larger headquarters building, a ten-story landmark on Wilshire Boulevard in Beverly Hills.

I continue to be involved with my friends. Dennis Hopper, a long-term guest with me in my Bel Air mansion in 1983, is now drug-free, as I am. I tried to help him when he was down. He has returned the favor by remaining a faithful and supportive ally. But two other close friends have died: Frank Zappa and Timothy Leary. Neither of these men can ever be replaced, and I feel their loss acutely.

It seems that prosecutors are finally weary of taking me to court. I have stayed out of the nation's courtrooms for several years now. The proliferation of sex on cable, satellite, and videocassettes has made the prosecution of *Hustler* more difficult. And compared to much that is available in print, on the Internet, and on television, *Hustler* is soft-core. The only trouble on the horizon at the moment is the new Communications Decency Act (part of the Federal Telecommunications Act). This legislation—which has received much press—is currently working its way through the lower courts, and most legal experts expect that it will eventually be ruled unconstitutional by the United States Supreme Court.

A steady stream of American and foreign journalists has passed through my office over the past few months. And they are using a new, friendlier vocabulary to describe me. Yet in my pain-free, drug-free mellowness, people are still not quite sure how to categorize me, and consequently they choose their adjectives carefully. A few have even dared to call me "respectable," even though they're not sure that they *want* to like me. For some people—particularly those who come with serious misgivings about my moral character—their unexpectedly positive impressions of me foment a moral crisis. It's as if they say to themselves, "Oh, my God, I like this man—what do I do now?" I have been a devil figure for so long that people have difficulty accepting the possibility that I might be a normal, rational human being. Yet I seem to be inching slowly toward some degree of respectability in the public consciousness. I don't expect *Time* magazine to nominate me "Man of the Year," nor do I expect the open embrace of mainstream America. I do, however, hope that Americans will grant me some small measure of credit—however grudgingly bestowed—for what I have done to protect their freedom of expression.

My inner life seems to have passed through three distinct phases. When I was a young man, I was idealistic and believed one individual could make a difference. "History depends on the intervention of great men and women," I thought. In my youth I dreamed of becoming wealthy and having an impact on the world. I committed every ounce of my energy and creativity to achieving that goal. After I was shot, I stopped dreaming. I had no goals beyond survival. Anger was the only emotion left; hope and optimism ceased to exist. Yet now I am neither as optimistic as in my youth, nor as angry as when I was in pain. I'm no longer sure anyone can make a real difference. I am no longer naive. But neither am I cynical. I live my life now in the hope of becoming a memory. I have put down the burden of trying to change the world and have decided to simply live life. There is a core of sadness in me—there always will be—but I have found happiness in the midst of my physical maladies, and in spite of the loss of Althea. Life goes on, and it is good.

Afterword

→

In early 1996 my business partner, Joel Gotler, came into my office and asked me whether I thought our literary agency ought to represent Larry Flynt. I could not understand why anyone would be interested in the life of such a reviled pornographer. My knowledge of this man was extremely limited: I knew he published *Hustler* magazine; that he had been shot and paralyzed; that he was reputed to be exceedingly difficult to work with. Why would a respectable literary agency want to represent him? End of story—or so I thought.

My curiosity got the better of me. I enjoy meeting people who are offbeat or notorious. Joel and I called Flynt's secretary and scheduled an appointment. To prepare for the meeting, I did some preliminary research on Flynt's life. Was there really enough interesting material to fill a book? I quickly found—to my surprise—that Flynt's life story is fascinating. In fact, as you now know, it is almost unbelievable. My reluctance turned into enthusiasm, and I soon found myself trying to convince others that this was a project worthy of representation, and deserving of publication.

The release of this book was an uphill battle. Every major publisher in New York turned down the opportunity to publish it. Their decision was based on the same limited perception and entrenched stereotype that I had originally shared. Larry Flynt was almost censored by ignorance and lack of curiosity. Ironically, those who had benefited the most from Larry Flynt's landmark First Amendment trials—America's publishing giants—were unwilling to print his story.

You, the reader, may have had your own doubts about Larry Flynt. But the mere fact that you have read this book separates you from the majority. I congratulate you for opening your mind and accepting the possibility that there might be something to be learned from this man's life. As you have seen in these pages, Larry Flynt has spent much of his career defending constitutional rights—rights that protect you and those around you.

Now that you have read the book, you still may not agree with certain actions Larry Flynt has taken. You may not like his strategy or his style; however, you may be less willing to attack him now that you understand where he has come from; how he grew up. You might even think that some of his actions were virtuous, and that some of his adversaries and critics were unscrupulous and hypocritical. Hopefully, you have found some of your perceptions of Larry Flynt changed, and have come to admire him at some level. If you have not, you should know this: Larry Flynt would be the first to defend your right to criticize him. Which is worse: the person who performs his deeds (or misdeeds) in public, or the one who secretly works behind the scenes to limit public freedoms?

—Alan Nevins
Renaissance Agency
Los Angeles, California